Alive and On Fire:
and other sermons that matter

Dana Vaughn

Parson's Porch Books
www.parsonsporchbooks.com

Alive and On Fire and other sermons that matter
ISBN: Softcover 978-1-949888-17-1
Copyright © 2018 by Dana Vaughn

All rights reserved. No part of this book may be reproduced or transmitted in any form or by any means, electronic or mechanical, including photocopying, recording, or by any information storage and retrieval system, without permission in writing from the publisher.

Alive and On Fire

Contents

Sermons Matter 7
The Abundant Life 9
   John 6:51-58
The Veil 16
   Exodus 34:29-35; Matthew 17:1-9
Alive and On Fire 23
   Jeremiah 20:7-13
An Inward Grace 29
   Matthew 3: 13-17
Easter People 35
   Mark 16:1-8
Get Up and Walk! 40
   John 5:1-9
God is Always with Us 47
   Isaiah 25:6-9; Romans 6:3-9
Honoring the Divine 54
   Matthew 22:34-46
Reconnect and Recharge 60
   Mark 6:30-34; 53-56
Stewardship: Investing in God 67
   Matthew 25:14-30
A Willingness to Serve 74
   1 Kings 17: 8-16
Fullness in God 80
   Hebrews 10:19-25 & Psalm 16
The Jericho Road 87
   Luke 10:25-37
The Lord of All 93
   Acts 10:34-43
The Power of Forgiveness 99
   Genesis 45:1-15; Matthew 15:10-20

Sermons Matter

Parson's Porch Books is delighted to present to you this series called Sermons Matter.

We believe that many of the best writers are pastors who take the role of preacher seriously. Week in, and week out, they exegete scripture, research material, write and deliver sermons in the context of the life of their particular congregation in their given community.

We further believe that sermons are extensions of Holy Scripture which need to be published beyond the manuscripts which are written for delivery each Sunday. Books serve as a vehicle for the sermon to continue to proclaim the Good News of the Morning to a broader audience.

We celebrate the wonderful occasion of the preaching event in Christian worship when the Pastor speaks, the People listen and the Work of the Church proceeds.

Take, Read, and Heed.

David Russell Tullock, M.Div., D.Min.
Publisher
Parson's Porch Books

The Abundant Life
John 6:51-58

A few years ago, a national survey was conducted to find out which phrase people desire to hear the most from other people. The overwhelming response for the top phrase people desire to hear the most from others was, "I love you." In a solid second place was, "I forgive you." And third place, which was a bit surprising was, "Dinner is ready."

This morning we encountered a text where Jesus is proclaiming that "Dinner is ready." He is essentially saying that He, Himself is the main course or entrée.

In this 6th chapter of John, we hear Jesus proclaiming to those who were gathered around Him that He is the bread of life. More specifically Jesus says:

> *I am the living bread that came down from heaven. Whoever eats this bread will live forever and the bread that I will give for the life of the world is my flesh.*

These verses can be somewhat off-putting for some people as they conjure up images of cannibalism, as Jesus speaks of literally eating His flesh, and drinking His blood.

He talks about how it is through eating His flesh and drinking His blood that we can gain life. That is why the Jews who were gathered around Jesus in this passage began to talk amongst themselves. They were questioning and disputing what Jesus was saying to them in this passage.

It started to raise questions for the Jews about *how* this man would give them His flesh to eat, and *why* Jesus would give them His flesh and blood to ingest.

After that, we see Jesus go into further detail about what He meant and what He was saying. More specifically, He says:

"Very truly I tell you unless you eat the flesh of the Son of Man and drink His blood you have no life in you. Those who eat my flesh and drink my blood have eternal life and I will raise them up on the last day."

Clearly, in this passage Jesus is not referring to the notion of cannibalism. But rather, Jesus is pointing to the action of Christ's saving grace on the cross. Pointing to the cross where Jesus' flesh will be broken for all of humanity. Where Jesus' blood will be poured out for all of mankind.

Jesus makes the association of how this violent death on the cross paves the way for the exact moment when Jesus will swap out His life for the life of the world. He underscores how it is through that action on the cross that will cause us, or allow us, to gain eternal life so that on our last day, He can raise us up, and we will gain our eternal union with God in heaven.

Going a step further here, the significance of what Jesus was saying in this passage is two-fold.

It is twofold in the sense that He tells us of how He came to offer His body and His blood so that we could gain eternal life, but it also tells us, of how Jesus came to offer up His flesh and blood so that we could gain life in the here and now.

This is not merely a text that reminds us of the hope of our faith—the hope of our eternal union with God. It is much richer than that. It is much richer than that as it invites us into full relationship with Jesus, now. It invites us into full participation in, and with, the life-giving power of Christ.

As we take Christ's body and blood into our mouths, into our stomachs, and into our bodies, either through; communion, through prayer, through coming to church, and all the other various ways, we impart Jesus into our lives and ingest Him in our bodies, then Christ remains in us, and we remain in Christ.

As we eat and drink Christ in, then Christ moves us closer to Himself. Christ moves us closer to the life of God. Christ moves us closer to Himself where we are as intimate with Jesus, as the Father is with the Son.

One Bible scholar wrote of it this way:

> Life according to this 6th chapter of John, means that what you need for your life to be sustained, God provides. That life is abundant, and that eternal life is not something you can conveniently and conventionally postpone to your future, but it is your promise in the present. Any claim about life, with Jesus or life with God, means an abiding, a unity, a reciprocity, a oneness with God now and forever. It means a real relationship in the here and now, that is not a remembrance of Jesus' past life or a hope for a future life, but life lived in the moment as God's grace upon grace is poured out upon us.

In the details of this passage, Jesus continually declares that dinner is ready, and that it is His flesh and His blood that are the main course. As He proclaims that message, there is one central theological claim to note in this passage, and that is, that Jesus came to give us life and to offer us abundant life.

Several years ago, I attended a Presbyterian Seminary in Richmond, VA. My 3-year seminary experience is not something I look back on fondly. I did make some great friends there, and I cherish that aspect of it, but Seminary was by far the most challenging academic program I ever endured. I found it to be, not only extremely academically challenging but, spiritually and even emotionally challenging.

Seminary challenges you in a way that no other college program does because as you are studying and learning more in depth about the field of theology and religion, it forces you to simultaneously analyze your own faith. It prompts you to unpack what you believe and really define the doctrines that undergird your faith and, that in turn, guide your entire life.

During my first year of seminary as I attended my theology classes and my old testament class, I found myself immersed in endless reading and thought about the various Christian doctrines of our faith. I was studying numerous theologians who had varying theories about the doctrines of our faith.

One theologian who I liked very much, and who had resonated with me and how I felt about God (my understanding of the Christian faith), would eventually end up contradicting another theologian, whom I may have equally liked what he/she had said about God and the Christian faith.

If I wasn't in class learning and talking about theology and discussing and interpreting scripture, then I was hanging out with friends having the same types of theological discussions. That is just the culture of a seminary campus. It's a thrilling good time.

About half way into my first year of seminary, after all these theological discussions and debates, and after months of studying various perspectives about the Christian faith, by many different theologians, I found myself in the midst of a faith crisis.

Somewhere along the way my personal religious views had become muddled by the overwhelming perspectives and various interpretations that I had read and heard about.

It skewed what I always thought to be true, and I found myself debating, even doubting, the central tenant of the Christian faith. I found myself doubting whether the resurrection and ascension of Christ had ever happened. More specifically, I found myself questioning how this pertained to me. Did Christ's death and ascensions have the power to affect me in any way?

This faith crisis coincided with the winter season when everything is dead and lifeless outside, which pretty much matched how I felt inside. It is quite miserable to experience a faith crisis. To question the things that you once believed so whole heartedly. It is quite miserable to start doubting and questioning those things that at one point had given you so much purpose and meaning, so much peace and joy and hope.

And on top of all that I felt like a fraud.

Here I was a seminary student, on track to become an ordained minister, and I possessed serious doubts about the central tenant of the Christian faith. So, as the days and weeks pressed on, I didn't tell anyone about what was going on with me and how I was enduring a terrible faith crisis. I hid how I felt and never vocalized what I was thinking, out of fear that I may get thrown out of seminary or that my ordination process would be derailed.

I just walked through it alone, and as I did, I kept reading more and more. I kept reading, and studying, and praying, as I tried to discern and define what I truly believed and why.

I remember one day during the dead of winter, amidst my faith crisis, I walked into the kitchen. At the time, I shared a house with several other people. One of my roommates was in there, and she asked me how I was doing. I told her I was fine. Then I asked her how she was doing. She said, "Oh, not good Dana, not good!" She said, "I am having a serious faith crisis."

When she spoke those words my heart about leapt out of my chest. Finally, I felt like I wasn't alone. Finally, I could tell someone what was really going on with me. I didn't have to hide my thoughts and feelings and keep them all bundled up inside any longer.

As I flipped around to look at her, and to tell her I was having a faith crisis too, she said, "yea I can't find my iPod anywhere, and I have looked everywhere!"

About that time, I felt a pit form in my stomach again. I thought to myself, "Well that's not exactly a faith crisis," and I went back to feeling miserable and very alone throughout that whole ordeal.

A few months later, spring finally arrived, and life was restored to the natural world again.

I could see the flowers blooming and popping up everywhere. There were leaves on the trees again. The birds were out singing. There was life and happiness all around!

As I watched this transformation within our natural world, where the natural world was turning from winter to spring, from death to life. It was that very action that began to spur on my belief in Christ again.

It made me realize that in just the same way that I didn't necessarily have all the answers, and understand the inner workings, of our natural world—how it can be so dead and lifeless for months on end and then suddenly spring back to life again. I also didn't have to have all the answers and fully understand the inner workings of Christ's death and resurrection, for it to be true and real.

It made me realize that below the surface of what we can see in our natural world, during those long cold snowy winter months, the trees the flowers the plants they are still alive. They are still active. They are still growing and preparing to bloom, at just the right moment.

And when spring comes, we see the visible signs of what was going on below the surface. Hidden from what the human eye can see.

Likewise, with the resurrection and ascension of Christ, there are many things that we cannot see. They are hidden from our human sight and understanding, but it doesn't negate what is going on below the surface, below what the human eye can see.

And we don't have to see it, understand it, and know all the answers to our questions, for it to be real and true. Because we can feel it.

I'll describe what I mean by that a little further.

During my faith crisis, I told you it was the dead of winter and when you are questioning God and your faith, and whether Christ really died for your sake. When you are questioning and doubting whether Christ really adds meaning to your life, you feel dead inside. There is no other way to say it or describe it. You feel dead inside. All joy, all happiness, all peace, and all hope for a brighter future is gone.

The moment that you start believing again and trusting that Jesus is who He says He is, life is restored to your body, to your mind, to your soul once again.

There are things about our faith that we cannot see. Things that we simply cannot understand and mysteries to our faith that we just simply must embrace.

What I can say, and what I gleaned from that experience was that whether we can explain it or not, whether we have all the answers or not, Christ was and is, and always will be, the true source of life for us.

He is the only source of life, or as John put in this passage, "Jesus is the living bread that came to give us all life." He came to give each of us abundant life, in the here and now *and* for all eternity.

In the name of the Father, the Son, and the Holy Spirit. Amen.

The Veil

Exodus 34:29-35; Matthew 17:1-9

Transfiguration Sunday

Today is Transfiguration Sunday. On Transfiguration Sunday, we celebrate the transfiguration of Christ and how Christ transfigured Himself before the disciples' eyes, thereby revealing His divine identity as God's Son to them and to the world.

As Jesus underwent this transfiguration, He had taken Peter, James and John up on top of a mountain to pray. While they were up there praying, He became transfigured. His physical appearance changed. His clothes became a bright and dazzling white. Then a cloud enveloped all of them, and God's voice cried out saying, "This is My Son, whom I have chosen, whom I love, listen to Him!"

The experience Jesus underwent, on that mountaintop with the disciples, reflects the same type of experience Moses had on Mount Sinai in our passage from Exodus. In those few verses from Exodus we heard how Moses came face-to-face with God at the top of Mount Sinai. After that face-to-face encounter when Moses came down off the mountain, he realized that he too had been transfigured up there on top of the mountain. He had been transfigured in such a way that his face was radiant. It shined brightly reflecting the light and Glory of God.

In fact, his face shined so brightly after that encounter with God that Moses had to place a veil over his face.

And that is what I wanted us to discuss a little bit further this morning. I wanted us to discuss the veil Moses wore after his face-to-face encounter with God, and how that veil relates to us in our own present day lives.

There are two points I would like to make regarding this veil. Two areas of significance.

The first area of significance regarding the veil is that it illustrates for us what happens when a person comes face-to-face with God.

The fact that Moses even had to wear a veil signifies how a person cannot encounter God without becoming transformed or transfigured in some way. One cannot come face-to-face with God without ending up a changed person forever.

This account may sound silly to modern ears, or perhaps you have at one point or another noticed the shiny face of someone else. Perhaps you have met someone who was very clearly radiating God's light and love and joy. Someone who was reflecting God's glory.

One of the first bits of astronomy we learn as children is that the moon, as large and as bright as it is, does not emit light of it's own. Instead, it's light is only a reflection of the sun's light and brilliance. In fact, the moon is only able to reflect 3-12% of the sun's light.

The same is the case for each of us. Each time we encounter God by spending time in prayer, reading scripture, or participating in a mission trip, it draws us into relationship with God. It brings us into contact with God. It allows us to have our own mountain top experience and come face-to-face with God.

When we experience those mountain top experiences with God, just like Jesus and Moses did in our passages, it changes us. It leaves a shiny and glowing radiance. Those face-to-face encounters with God allow us to walk away from that experience impacted in such a way where we are transformed. As a result, we can't help but to reflect God's light.

That is the first point of significance regarding Moses's veil. Moses' veil informs us of what happens when we come face-to-face with God. His veil reminds us how each encounter with God leaves us changed and transformed in deep and impactful ways. Each face-to-face encounter with God leaves us transformed in such a way where we can't help but to radiate God's light for others to see.

The second point of significance regarding Moses veil is that it illustrates how we sometimes want to mask ourselves in front of other people.

Moses' veil illustrates how we put up barriers which prevent others from being able to fully see and experience the light and glory of God, that we are intended to reflect.

When Moses came down that mountain, he had no clue he was so shiny and glowing so brightly. He just went about his normal life doing what he typically would have done. He came down the mountain and delivered the Ten Commandments to the Israelites like God had instructed him to do. It was in that moment that he learned how shiny his face was. In that moment, he learned how he had been transfigured during that face-to-face encounter with God.

As Moses learned how shiny and bright he was, he saw how other people responded to him and the reactions they were having towards him. He saw how people were frightened by his physical appearance and how they were scared to come around him. He watched as they recoiled in his presence.

So, what did Moses do as he witnessed these types of reactions?

He veiled himself.

He put a mask or a veil over his face to hide the radiant glow of God. He put a veil over his face so that he was no longer reflecting God's light and glory. So as to not scare people off. So that he wasn't deemed weird and transfigured or different from everyone else.

This event speaks to us today. It represents how we veil our own faces and how we mask ourselves when it comes to sharing God's light with other people or radiating God's glow for others to see. It signifies how we hesitate to share stories about our faith with other people. We shy away from talking about God in our daily affairs. It illustrates how we don't openly express our faith with others out of fear of how they may react to us.

Moses' use of a veil drives home the point of how we put up our own barriers or masks, and veil ourselves so we don't scare people off, so we aren't deemed weird or different from others because of our faith.

A couple years ago, I was at a Christian education conference. During that conference, I was provided with some interesting and alarming statistics regarding the decline of church membership within in the Presbyterian denomination, as well as the overall decline in church participation throughout all protestant churches.

These are some of the statistics that I learned at that time about the decline in protestant churches across the board:

1. Every year 2.7 million church members fall into the inactive status.

2. Every year more than 4,000 churches close their doors.

3. From 1990 to 2000 the combined membership of all Protestant denominations in the US declined by almost 5 million members, while the U.S. population increased by 24 million people. That gives us some insight into the distorted proportions.

4. The United States now ranks third (3rd) following China and India in the number of people who are not professing Christians. In other words, the U.S. is becoming an ever increasing "un-reached or un-churched group of individuals."

5. Just 18% of Americans report they attended church "frequently" and only 11% go to church regularly.

Here are a couple of statistics regarding the Presbyterian denomination specifically:

1. In 2011, the denomination experienced a decline of 63,804 members and had a loss of 96 congregations in that same year.

2. The overall PCUSA membership is now down to 1.76 million people. That is the global membership which is down almost 3/4 of a million people from 2006.

Many speculate why there has been such a steady and consistent decrease in church membership and participation. The key note speaker at that conference had an interesting perspective she shared.

Lilian Daniel was the keynote speaker, and after sharing these alarming statistics with us this is what she said:

She said, "This is to be expected since we now live in a culture where we no longer talk about God or our faith. We no longer talk to other people about what God is doing in our lives. Instead, we talk about the weather, or current events, or we gossip about other people. Instead we talk about shows and sitcoms."

She said, "We have turned into a culture that is much more laid back when it comes to sharing our faith. If we do talk about God, or our faith, then it is conveyed as do whatever floats your boat or do whatever is going to make you happy."

She went on to say, "those who are actually talking about their faith come from a very strict conservative religious background. They convey a fire and brimstone message and impress upon others the importance of accepting Jesus in their lives, so they don't burn in hell for all eternity."

"Therefore," Lilian said, "We must adopt an attitude where we have something to say between fire and brimstone and do whatever makes you happy or do whatever floats your boat."

Gradye Parsons who was the stated clerk for the PCUSA in 2012 had a similar statement regarding the decline in membership and overall participation in the Presbyterian church.

He said (and I am paraphrasing), "The first and primary need is to continue to increase our efforts to live out the Great Commission and share the Good News of Jesus Christ. Those statistics challenge us as Presbyterians to re-connect with the ever-growing number of those who have no religious affiliation. Those who deem and title themselves as spiritual but not-religious, and to talk to them about our faith. To not be fearful to talk to them and all others about how we are experiencing God in our day-to-day lives."

Both of those individuals make valid points.

One of the most essential tenets of our faith is to go out into the world and *share* the Good News of Christ with others. Friends, we cannot do that if we keep our faces veiled. We cannot share the Good News of Christ with others if we are not willing to step-outside of our comfort zone, take our veils off, and share stories about our faith with others.

One of the key parts of our faith is helping others to see and experience God in their lives, and we do that by talking about God, by manifesting God's presence for others to feel and experience. We do that by reflecting God's light and glory for others to see.

Moses's veil reminds us how easy it is to mask ourselves. How easy it can become to put up a barrier between ourselves and other people and hide our faith from other people.

These alarming statistics that I shared with you show us what the consequences are for putting that veil over our faces, and for becoming too afraid to share our faith with other people.

These alarming statistics show us what the consequences are for being a laid-back culture where people no longer talk about God and faith in their day-to-day interactions, but instead adopt an attitude of do whatever makes you happy do whatever floats your boat.

So, as we consider the two things Moses's veil represents and what those two things signify in our own personal lives, then there are four questions for further introspection:

1. In what ways have you encountered God in your personal life?

2. In what significant ways have we come face-to-face with God?

3. How has that face-to-face encounter with God changed you and impacted you? How has that face-to-face encounter with God left you transfigured with your own radiant glow?

4. Are you willing to share that story with other people? Are you willing to reflect the light and glory of God throughout your day-to-day lives as you interact with people?

The big question from this passage is whether we are willing to remove our own veils, and masks, and go out into the world to tell others about God. To share stories of our faith with others, and even invite them to come to church so they can experience it for themselves.

There are times when it is easier to shy away from sharing our faith with others, telling others about our faith, and reflecting God's light for others to see. Today, we were reminded of what happens when we veil ourselves in this way and when we don't let the light and glory of God shine brightly.

We were reminded of the alarming number of people who aren't hearing about and encountering God's light and glory anymore.

Those numbers are going to continue to grow and church participation will continue to decline, if we don't start removing our veils and start sharing stories about God and our faith more often.

On this Transfiguration Sunday, we are reminded of the importance of removing our masks our veils, and any other barriers, so that we can truly reflect the light and glory of God for all to see.

In the name of the Father, the Son, and the Holy Spirit. Amen.

Alive and On Fire
Jeremiah 20:7-13

When I first realized that God was calling me to seminary, and as I answered that call, there were a variety of responses that I received from my friends and family.

My immediate family was somewhat surprised by my decision. At that point in my life I was enrolled in a Ph.D. program for counseling, so my family was highly surprised to hear that I was transferring out of my counseling program and into seminary, but overall my family was supportive and encouraging.

When my close circle of friends heard that I was going to seminary, many of them had no clue what that meant, and several of them thought it entailed heading off to live in the mountains where I would be taking a vow of silence for the next three years.

And then I had a couple of other friends who ended our friendship when they heard I was going to seminary. They ended our friendship because they didn't believe that a woman should have a leadership role in the church or that a female should be seeking ordination.

So, there was a variety of responses from people—some positive some negative, and some were just not sure what answering a call and heading to seminary really entailed. And in all honesty, at that point in my life, I don't think I fully knew what to expect or fully knew what seminary would entail.

Despite the criticism I received, and the negative comments made to me about attending seminary, and seeking ordination as a female, I knew with certainty that God had placed a call on my life, and I knew there would be a restlessness in my soul until I answered that calling. So, I left for seminary and headed off to live in the big city of Richmond, Virginia.

As I left for seminary there were several things I left behind. I left behind:

- A full-time job as a counselor, and a part time job as a youth director. In other words, I left behind steady income and financial stability.

- The comforts of living in the same hometown as my immediate family. Which entailed the freedom to pop in and visit with family members anytime I wanted and the ability to get together with family for every holiday birthday or impromptu cookout.

- The luxury of living in my own town-home in the suburbs of Roanoke, Virginia

When I arrived at seminary, I embarked on a new journey which entailed:

- Moving into small on-campus housing. And I mean small, like one bedroom and a bathroom that you shared with your suite-mate kind of small. Sharing a kitchen with 14 other people. So nice and small communal living, at the age of 28.

- Moving to a city that was 3 hours away from my immediate family, and a crime ridden city at that. My new neighborhood was no exception. There were shootings, gang activity, and assaults that occurred on my block regularly. Including a shooting that took place directly out front of my window during my last year of seminary.

- No longer being able to work full time. Instead, I had to take out student loans to make ends meet. So, there was no financial stability or steady income.

There were times when I first got to seminary, and for probably about the first year and half, in which I thought, "What in the world have I done?"

So, when I read this passage of Jeremiah, and when I hear this part of Jeremiah's call story, where he struggled with answering God's call, it always resonates with me. It resonates with me because I feel like I really get Jeremiah. I feel like I really understand the struggles Jeremiah faced as he wrestled with answering God's call. Mostly because I too wrestled and struggled with the call that God had placed on my life. However, Jeremiah had it a whole lot worse

God called Jeremiah to go and preach a message of destruction to the inhabitants of Jerusalem. To warn the people living there that their city would be destroyed. As you might imagine that message did not make Jeremiah a popular man or a well-liked person. This message God called him to deliver made him a laughing stock, and everyone mocked him, even his close friends looked down upon him and abandoned him.

Jeremiah was not thrilled about what God had called him to do. In this text you can hear Jeremiah lashing out at God, but nevertheless he still did what God asked him to do. He still went and preached this message of destruction and answered God's call. He did it because he said that it felt as if there was a fire burning within him that he could not contain. A burning fire shut up in his bones that he could not conceal.

Jeremiah couldn't help but to go and deliver this message and do what God had asked, which is another reason why Jeremiah's call story personally resonates with me so much. When I first answered God's call and headed to seminary, I went there to gain the theological and religious education I needed in order to work in ministry.

The part of ministry I always foresaw myself working in was youth ministry, and I imagined I would continue providing counseling, since that was the type of work I had been doing before I headed off to seminary.

The only part of ministry that I was adamant about not doing was solo pastor work. Clearly, God had other plans for my life because I have now been working as a solo pastor for close to 5 years.

It was during my second year of seminary as I continued to discern my call to full time ministry that I realized God was calling me to solo pastor work.

As part of my discernment process at that time, I spent a lot of my time in prayer and reflecting. I also spent a lot of time outside in nature running or jogging.

One day while I was out running, I saw a car with a license plate that said: JER 20:9. I had no clue what that verse said so I made a mental note to make sure I looked up Jeremiah chapter 20 verse 9 when I got home.

When I got home, I forgot to look it up.

About a week later, I was driving down the interstate, and I saw a billboard on the side of the road that said the same thing Jeremiah 20:9. So, I thought well that's strange to see this verse listed again, and I made another mental note to look it up when I got home.

Well, when I got home, I forgot again.

The following week I went to chapel, on campus, like I did every Wednesday during seminary. As I looked over the bulletin to see which passages, we would be reading, I saw the Old Testament Passage was Jeremiah chapter 20 verses 7-13 (which includes Jeremiah 20 verse 9).

So, God had my attention at that point: I was all ears. Once I heard this passage from Jeremiah read, and, more specifically, once I heard Jeremiah 20 verse 9, when Jeremiah describes this fire burning within him which he couldn't contain—a fire that was shut up in his bones—I felt as if it described my own faith.

Throughout my entire life I had been exposed to various life events that had awakened me to God's presence in my life. Certain life events they had allowed me to truly experience God's love and grace and mercy in a deep and palpable way.

That type of visceral encounter with God's grace and mercy and love had created a burning desire within me to share those things with other people.

Essentially, I had come alive in Christ and was on fire to share Christ's love and grace with everyone I encountered. I wanted other people to be able to experience those same things. For them to be just as excited about God and their faith as I was.

So, after hearing this passage read during our chapel service that day, I realized that I couldn't keep that burning feeling within, and that I needed to be completely open to God's call on my life, wherever it may have led me and whatever form it may take on. Even if that meant working as a solo pastor.

As it turns out, the very last thing I ever envisioned myself doing, and the very thing I was adamant about not doing, is exactly what God was calling me to do, and it is exactly what I love doing.

I have told people before I love what I do so much, that I would do it for free. I am so passionate about what I do that it never feels like work; it never leaves me drained. Instead, I feel like I am constantly re-invigorated by what I do day in and day out.

God places a call on each and every single one of our lives, and each call is individually based. God's call is not just for ordained ministry alone, but God's call may consist of being a full-time care giver for a parent or a loved one. For another person, it may mean watching over or helping to raise your grandchild. God's call may entail volunteering at a local agency or volunteering at the church. God calls each and every single one of us in very different ways.

Sometimes in life, God calls us to do things that we never would have imagined ourselves doing. Sometimes God calls us to do things that are difficult and that we struggle with. Sometimes God calls us to do things that don't make us popular or well-liked amongst our friends.

Despite how difficult those calls may be at the time, God promises to always be with us, to never abandon or forsake us.

Our passages this morning highlights how God calls each of us to do certain things which are hard things that we may never have envisioned ourselves doing. Sometimes God calls us to do things what we don't want to do, but we do not struggle to answer God's call alone.

God is with us every step of the way. God equips us with exactly what we need at the exact moment we need it, so we can accomplish the task at hand.

Life as a Christian is not always serene. It is not always a quiet submission to God's will. But rather, often times it is a life of struggle with God, and a struggle to stay in-line with God's will for our lives.

May we all open ourselves up to God's call in our lives, whatever form that call may take on, or wherever that call may lead us. May we trust that no matter how difficult God's call is in our lives, God is with us every step of the way, equipping us with exactly what we need.

May we all come alive in Christ, with a burning fire within us to share God's love and grace and mercy with all others.

In the name of the Father, the Son and the Holy Spirit. Amen!

An Inward Grace
Matthew 3: 13-17

Our Gospel reading this morning told of the time when John the Baptist baptized Jesus in the Jordan river. Unlike Jesus who was baptized at a much older age, within the Presbyterian denomination we baptize children at infancy.

The theology behind this practice of infant baptism signifies our belief that God is present in our lives from the very beginning. Infant baptism signifies our awareness of how God is at work in our lives well before we even have the capability of comprehending it. Our practice of infant baptism represents our belief and awareness of how there is nothing we can do to earn God's love and grace.

In much the same way that a child is not able to earn their parents love and grace; it is freely bestowed upon them. God's love and grace is a gift that is freely bestowed upon us.

Since the Presbyterian way of doing things entails baptizing children at infancy, then that means that those who have grown up in the Presbyterian church do not have the privilege of remembering their own baptism. They may see pictures or hear stories about it, but they aren't able to recall it on their own.

I know that some of you are cradle Presbyterians. You have been part of the Presbyterian Church since day one, which means you aren't able to recall your baptism and how you felt that day as you became a newly baptized child of God.

Others of you have a Baptist upbringing, and you experienced your baptism in a different way where you were much older when you were baptized, and you do have the ability to recall that special day and event.

I did not grow up in the Presbyterian Church, therefore I was not baptized as an infant, so I do have the luxury and privilege of recalling my own baptism. I can remember what it was like that day and how I felt afterwards.

As a young girl I attended a Baptist church, not too far from my home, and at age 10, I was baptized in that church. On the day of my baptism, I remember wearing all white as I had been instructed to do so by my pastor.

When we reached the point in our service when I was to be baptized, I remember walking up to the front of the sanctuary and climbing into a huge tub of water that was on the chancel. At that point, my pastor said a few words, had a prayer, and then I was fully submerged into the tub of water three times as he said, "In the name of the Father, the Son, and the Holy Spirit."

Afterwards, everyone was smiling and clapping, and I was eventually led off the chancel to a back room where I changed into some dry clothes and blow dried my hair.

As I was in that back room changing and getting ready, I remember inspecting myself as if there was supposed to be some sort of change in my physical appearance. I kept studying myself in the mirror, and since I didn't see any physical changes in my appearance, I got dressed, and I marched right out of that back room and straight over to mom and said, "Mom, I don't think we did it right. I don't look any different!"

My mom snickered and then she reassured me that my baptism had gone exactly like it was supposed to. She told me that it wasn't supposed to cause any changes in my outer appearance, but rather it was more about how I was creating a relationship with God. It was more about the changes that were occurring inside of me, as a result.

For months after my baptism, and despite what my mother had told me about my baptism, I was absolutely convinced that my pastor hadn't baptized me correctly. It wasn't until several years later that I really understood what my mother meant and what my baptism signified. As the years passed on, I did start to experience changes in my life because of my baptism.

They weren't changes to my physical appearance like I had anticipated as a 10-year-old girl, but there were some pivotal changes that occurred with my inner identity and how I perceived myself.

In the years following my baptism, I came to understand myself in a new and different way where I was no longer just Dana Vaughn, the daughter of David and Bettegene Vaughn, but rather I was Dana Vaughn, the daughter of God.

And as that child of God I knew that God loved me. God was always watching over me and providing for me. I knew that God had a plan and purpose for my life. All of which made me a stronger and more confident young woman.

That is precisely what our baptism is supposed to do. It is supposed to change and effect our inner identity. How we perceive ourselves and who we understand ourselves to be. It gives us direction in life and the inner strength we need to persevere during times of difficulty. It instills an inner confidence within us that can never be shaken.

Our baptism changes and effects how we relate to the world, and how we live and interact with other people.

St. Augustine once described the sacrament of baptism as an outward and visible sign, of an inward and invisible grace.

Now that may sound like a very simple answer, but it points to the complexity of the Christian journey. After our baptism, we spend our entire lives journeying closer to God and working to further the kingdom of God here on earth.

St. Augustine's description of baptism points to the inner awakening we experience at our baptism and the grace we receive which then compels us, throughout our entire lives, to follow in Christ's footsteps and continuously nudges us throughout our lives to live as Christ did, at all costs.

Dietrich Bonhoeffer, the brilliant German theologian, wrote a book on this topic called, *The Cost of Discipleship*. One of the most quoted parts of the book deals with the distinction which Bonhoeffer makes between "cheap grace" and "costly grace".

According to Bonhoeffer, "'cheap grace" is the preaching of forgiveness without requiring repentance or baptism without church discipline? Or having Communion without confession. According to Bonhoeffer Cheap grace is grace without discipleship. Grace without the cross grace without Jesus Christ."

Cheap grace, Bonhoeffer says, "is to hear the gospel preached as follows: of course, you have sinned but now everything is forgiven, so you can stay as you are and enjoy the consolations of forgiveness."

Bonhoeffer says the main defect of such a proclamation is that it contains no demand for discipleship.

In contrast to cheap grace, "costly grace" confronts us with a gracious call to follow Jesus. It is costly because it compels a man to submit to the yoke of Christ and follow him.

Recently, a congregation was present for the baptism of a 55-year-old man who had just started coming to church. His first questions were, "What do I have to do to be baptized, and what is going to happen to me afterwards?"

On the day of this man's baptism, the bishop stood at the font and the man bowed his head as the priest poured water on him and anointed him.

Afterward he shared how moving the experience had been for him. He told the story of how something had always been missing in his life. He had been a counselor until retirement, and he now realized the wholeness given to him just as he had often tried to help others find it in their own lives.

He is now a volunteer at a food pantry and on Christmas Day he offered to help cook and serve Christmas dinner for others at a local health clinic. He spent Christmas weekend with his family but on Christmas Day he feed and took care of others.

At the point of our baptism, there is an inner awakening that compels us to follow in Christ's footsteps and nudges us to live as Christ did at all costs.

There are certain times in our lives when we may feel more compelled to follow in Christ's footsteps and more compelled to live as Christ did, than at other points in our lives. That is all just part of the Christian journey. But nevertheless, there is always an inward grace at work within us. A divine stirring, nudging us and shaping us into Christ's disciples.

I heard a story recently about a woman who found herself being prodded to do something about the lack of housing for the poor and homeless in her community. Among them were undocumented people who were out of work; single mothers with children and several who were simply alone.

She tried to get the attention of her church about their plight. A committee was formed but nothing happened. Then she decided to take matters into her own hands and began meeting with the people themselves.

They organized a housing co-operative and before long they found a small vacant motel they could buy. Having no funds, they began to search for resources, and through a process of diligent work and generosity, they put together a financial package to buy the motel.

They found a man willing to be their residential manager and now on cold winter nights, and in the heat of summer, several dozen people have housing. Her church has now become an integral part of the enterprise as well.

The sacrament of baptism may not have an outward effect on us. We may not look any different when we look at ourselves in the mirror, but it most certainly has an inward effect on us.

There is an inward grace at work within each of us that compels us to live and act differently in this world. There is an inward effect that nudges us to submit to the yoke of Christ and to follow Him.

The next time you find yourself witnessing the act of baptism, allow that time to be a moment of re-affirmation for you. Allow that time to be a moment when you re-affirm your own baptismal vows as those questions are asked.

Questions like: Do you profess Jesus Christ to be your Lord and Savior and will you be Christ's faithful disciple obeying His word and show His love?

As you hear those same vows again, may you all take a moment to silently reflect on your own baptism and where your baptismal journey has led you over the years.

May it be a time where we open ourselves up to that inward grace once again, that divine stirring within. May we be awakened to that inner nudge that compels us to follow in Christ's footsteps and live as Christ did, at all costs.

In the name of the Father, the Son, and the Holy Spirit. Amen.

Easter People
Mark 16:1-8

Easter

A wise man once said to me, "There are times in life in which we experience death, but there always is a resurrection."

This man was not talking about experiencing a literal death, but rather he was speaking about those events in our lives that make us feel as if a part of us has died. He was referring to those traumas in life that cause us to suffer and feel heart-wrenching pain.

He was pointing out how regardless of how much suffering and heart wrenching pain we endure, death never has the final word. There is always a resurrection!

That is the truth and beauty of Easter. The truth is, there will be a bloody and painful death on Good Friday, and the beauty is that come Easter morning, there will be a glorious resurrection!

We are Easter people following a resurrected Christ, and the truth and beauty of Easter is as relevant for our lives, as it was for Christ many centuries ago.

There are difficulties we face in life that inflict deep wounds upon us and setbacks that are absolutely devastating, hardships that rob us of our joy. Pain and suffering are inevitable in life, but death never speaks the last word to us.

Our God is a God of resurrection power and is always creating new life out of death. God always has a plan to take the broken pieces of our lives and make something beautiful with them. God's intention is always to bind up our brokenness and make us whole again.

Vance Havner, a well-known Baptist minister, once said "God uses broken things: Broken soil to produce a crop, broken clouds to give rain, broken grain to give bread, and broken bread to give strength.

It is the broken alabaster box that gives forth perfume. It is Peter weeping bitterly who returns to greater power than ever."

God meet us in our brokenness in the most broken places of our lives, and in the most broken areas of our heart and creates a resurrection story.

There was a segment on CBS Sunday Morning that I watched several years ago. It was about a man name Nick Voy-chitch. You all may be familiar with his story or his NY best seller book, *Unstoppable*.

Nick was born in Melbourne, Australia without arms or legs and was given no medical reason for this condition. His mother stated she took every precaution during the pregnancy. She didn't even drink coffee or tea.

Nick, who is now 31, faced countless challenges and obstacles while growing up. At age 6, he was given prosthetic limbs to help him adapt, but later he refused them and said he was better off without them. He continued trying to keep up with everyone else. He taught himself how to cook, how to skateboard, and how to play ball with his head.

Despite all he did to try and keep up with everyone else, the curious looks turned into bully. At age 8, the bullying resulted in Nick coming home nearly every day from school crying. Most days when his parents would drop him off at school, he would refuse to go in or would hide in the gardens. At age 10, Nick attempted suicide.

During bath time, Nick asked his father to leave him in there alone for a while. When his father shut the door, Nick slid beneath the water and rolled over face down. As he laid there under the water attempting to drown himself, he saw an image of his mother and father, and brother standing over his grave crying, and he couldn't do it.

After that Nick learned to embrace his disability and found a way around almost every obstacle. He can now type 60 words a minute, he swims, surfs, skydives, and restores old cars.

He travels all around the world as a motivational speaker and evangelist. He has traveled to over 60 countries and to countless schools, churches, prisons, orphanages, hospitals, and stadiums within the states sharing his story and personal testimony. In 2005, Nick created a foundation called *Life Without Limbs* which focuses on helping others who are suffering with their own silent troubles.

Nick stated during an interview, "I have seen the grace of God. I have seen him take even the most broken pieces of my life and make it into something beautiful. I think I went through that so I could share that story with the world because there are a lot of hurting people out there."

The segment ended by showing clips of Nick at his wedding reception dancing with his wife. At the very end of the interview, he announced the news that they fell pregnant after the honeymoon and that the sonograms show the child does have 10 fingers and 10 toes.

Our God is a God of resurrection power and is always creating new life out of death. God always has a plan to take the broken pieces of our lives and make something beautiful with them. God's intention is always to bind up our brokenness and make us whole again.

Warren Wiersbe wrote a book called, *Victorious Christian*. It is about Fanny Crosby who is the author of over 8,000 songs including several that are found in church hymnals. In fact, she wrote so many that she had to write under pseudonyms, just so she could get more of her songs into the hymnbooks.

At 6 weeks of age, Fanny Crosby developed a minor eye inflammation and was taken to a local doctor for treatment. However, the doctor who treated her used the wrong medicine on her eyes and she became totally and permanently blind because of his carelessness.

Interviewed years later, Fanny Crosby said she harbored no bitterness against the physician. In fact, she once said, "If I could meet him now, I would say thank you over and over again for making me blind." She felt that her blindness was a gift from God to help her write the hymns that flowed from her pen.

Our encounters with the resurrection power of God may not be quite as elaborate or dramatic as Nick Voy-Chitch's or Fanny Crosby's story, but we all have our own resurrection story. We have all experienced God meeting us in the brokenness of our lives and watched Him generate new life, new beginnings, and new possibilities for us.

The resurrection power of God that we experience on Easter morning is not just something we joyfully celebrate once a year, but it's something we experience all throughout our lives. God always has a resurrection story in mind for each of us.

Having been born and raised in the south never living a day in my life above the Mason Dixon line until I moved to western New York, I had a much different encounter with the events of Holy Week.

This year as I prepared for Holy week and anticipated Easter, I was captivated by how closely our natural world here in the frozen North acts as a metaphor for Holy Week.

We endure extremely cold winters here. The total average snowfall is far greater than any amount of snow I have ever witnessed in all my years combined. Close to 200 inches of snow each winter.

And you guys' winter last forever. In the South spring has already sprung. The Bradley Pear Trees have already sprouted their white flowers. The cherry blossoms and the dogwoods are in full bloom. People are most likely already laying outside tanning!

So, as I took notice of our natural world over the past week and a half, and witnessed the snow receding and life returning to earth's surface, I couldn't help but think about how it perfectly symbolized the events of Holy Week.

During these long and cold winters that we endure, everything seems so dead and lifeless outside. The leaves fall off the trees making our world so barren and colorless. The snow blankets the land and stays for an eternity. There were some places here in Westfield where the ground was frozen more than 41 inches below the earth's surface that's over 3 feet!

Yet when the snow finally does recede and melts away, there is life under there after all, and one can immediately see the green daffodil buds breaking through the ground.

All the while we were enduring this long cold winter, our natural world below the surface is still very much at work. It is still very active and generating new life; we just couldn't see it quite yet.

Similarly, this is what we experience during Holy Week. On Good Friday we experience the cold death of our Lord, but by Sunday morning we experience new life as our Lord is raised from the dead.

And we encounter the same thing in our own personal lives as well. There are long agonizing deaths we face at certain times in our lives. Traumas that leave us feeling somewhat lifeless, and we feel as if the pain lasts for an eternity. But all the while we're enduring that long agonizing death, God is working below the surface generating new life, with plans to raise us up.

The Apostle Paul's words to the Ephesians are exceedingly appropriate for us this morning. Paul says,

> *"I also pray that you will understand the incredible greatness of God's power for us who believe him. This is the same mighty power that raised Christ from the dead and seated him in the place of honor at God's right hand in the heavenly realms."*

Ephesians adds to our astonishment this Easter morning. The "mighty power that raised Christ from the dead", is in fact, "God's power for us who believe in him"

While we celebrate the resurrection power of God on this Easter Sunday, let us rejoice in knowing that that same power is available to each and every single one of us.

That no matter what trials and tribulations we may face in life, death never speaks the last word! There always is a resurrection story!

Thanks be to God that we are Easter people and that we always have the message of the resurrection to hold on to!

In the name of the Father, the Son, and the Holy Spirit. Amen!

Get Up and Walk!
John 5:1-9

In our passage from John this morning we heard Jesus ask a man, who had been ill for 38 years, if he wanted to be made well again.

This seems like a fairly odd question to ask someone who has been sick for so long. It seems like Jesus would have already known the answer to that question.

And it's also an odd question to ask someone who is lying beside a pool waiting to be miraculously healed by its waters. It seems like you would be able to tell that person is willing to go to whatever lengths it takes to be healed.

While this question may seem somewhat odd and mysterious, the pool itself remained a mystery for many years. For centuries, scholars believed there was no such pool because there was no sign of it in modern-day Jerusalem. So, for the longest time this story was treated as a metaphor, rather than an actual account with a historical location.

However, in the 19th century, an archaeologist by the name of Schick discovered a pool, which he contended was the pool from John 5. Further excavation in 1964, revealed other features that confirmed that it was in fact this pool.

But here's the piece I find most interesting: the pool was also used as an Asklepion, an ancient healing temple. A place where healing was supposed to take place by the power of Asclepius, the Greek god of healing. Asclepius was even called, "savior" by his followers.

According to this explanation, people believed this Greek god would come and stir the waters in the healing temple, and that whoever was the first to enter the pool, after the waters had been stirred, would be healed of his or her malady.

Therefore, the pool and the surrounding area had become the gathering place for anyone with any sort of sickness. Especially the blind, the lame, and the paralyzed. They all gathered there watching the surface of the water, waiting for this Greek god to cause the smallest ripple in the waters, so they could jump in and be healed.

So, while it may seem like an odd question for Jesus to ask a man, who had been sick for 38 years, if he wanted to be made well, what Jesus was really asking him was, "Do you want to believe in the real savior, not just a Greek god who people call savior?"

While it may seem odd for Jesus to ask a man who is lying beside a healing pool if he wants to be healed, what Jesus was really asking him was, "Do you want to trust in something that actually works and has the power to heal you and not just sit here and wait for some waters to stir?"

Now the man's response to Jesus' question was equally puzzling as well. When Jesus asked this man if he wanted to be made well, we would expect to hear a resounding, "Yes" from him. After all he has been sick for so long. However, when this guy responded, he offered a couple of complaints or a couple obstacles as to why he couldn't be healed.

He says, "Sir I have no one to put me into the pool when the water is stirred up. Then he says, "and while I am making my way someone else steps down ahead of me."

It appears as if, what is standing in the way of this man's healing is himself. It appears as if it's his own negative thinking that is preventing him from being healed. It appears as if it's his own negative thinking about his situation, his disbelief in himself, and his disbelief in what Jesus can do for him.

And at this point in the story Jesus then tells the man to get up, grab his mat, and walk.

Now this may seem like a harsh response to command someone who has been sick for 38 years, to stand up, grab his stuff, and walk on but there is significance in Jesus words.

The first part of the significance in Jesus' words lies in Jesus telling him, to get up! The Greek word that is used here to command the man to get up can be translated as rise or stand, but it can also be translated as, *awaken!*

So, Jesus wasn't trying to be rude or harsh to the man, rather he was telling him *to awaken* from all this disbelief in himself, and this negative way of thinking that had left him sick for 38 years.

To awaken from this absurd belief that a Greek god was his savior and was going to come down and save him by stirring some waters that would magically heal him.

Instead, Jesus was telling him *to awaken* to a new positive way of thinking. To believe in himself, to trust in God for healing, and to awaken to what all God could achieve with him and through him.

There are times in our lives when it is easy for us to be this man. It is easy to slip into a mindset of negative thinking about ourselves or about what God can do in our lives or whether God can improve what seems like an impossible situation for us.

We are reminded this morning of the power of God, and we're asked to awaken to a more positive way of thinking where we believe in ourselves, where we trust and believe in all the great things that God can do with us and through us.

Recently, I stumbled upon some inspirational information about some top celebrities who have experienced obstacles in their own life, but they still went on to do big and great things.

I wanted to share this information with you because it helps us to see how all of us face obstacles and difficulties in life and how those things don't have to hamper or hinder us from moving forward and achieving great things.

At age 23, Oprah was devastated when she was fired from her first reporting job, but that didn't stop her, she is now a media mogul, owns her own television network and is worth billions.

At age 23, Tina Fey was working at a YMCA, now she has a net worth of $45 million.

At age 24, Stephen King was working as a janitor and living in a trailer.

At age 27, Vincent Van Gogh failed as a missionary and decided to go to art school.

At age 28, J.K. Rowling was a suicidal single parent living on welfare, now she has written over 13 books including, *The Harry Potter* series.

At age, 30 Harrison Ford was a carpenter.

Vera Wang failed to make the Olympic figure skating team, then she didn't get the Editor-in-Chief position at Vogue, but she went on to design her first dress at age 40. She now has her own multimillion-dollar clothing line and is branching out into jewelry design as well.

Samuel L. Jackson didn't get his first movie role until he was 46.

Morgan Freeman landed his first major movie role at age 52.

Grandma Moses didn't begin her painting career until age 76.

Louise Bourgeois didn't become a famous artist until she was 78.

Moral of the story: Never tell yourself that you aren't good enough, or that you missed your chance. Never let an obstacle stand in the way of moving forward and dreaming big about what God can do with you and through you.

This morning we are reminded to awaken to a more positive way of thinking where we believe in ourselves, where we trust and believe in all the great things that God can do with our lives.

We are invited to dream big about what God has in store for us or what we would like to see happen with our lives, and as you dream big about these things, be prepared to put some work into it.

Those celebrities didn't hit an obstacle and give up. They worked hard to get where they are today. Oprah Winfrey arose from poverty, abuse, and prejudice to become one of the most influential people on the planet. After being fired from her first reporting job, she now earns an annual salary of $315 million.

In order to do great things, there is work involved, and that is the other significant part about what Jesus said to the man by the pool.

After Jesus commanded this man to get up, to awaken to all these new possibilities for his life, Jesus then told him to walk!

Essentially what Jesus was saying to the man was, to move and start doing work. Now that his man was cured of his illness, he was going to have to get a job, he was going to have to support his family, he was going to have to give back to society in some way. Essentially, he was going to have to walk around and conduct his life.

William Sloane Coffin a great minister and peace activist once said, "It is certainly scarier to be cured from an illness, than to be sick because if you are cured then you become responsible, which means that you are response-able. Able to respond to God's call, able to respond to the word, able to cease being a victim, and share the love of Christ with others."

When you become response-able you must work hard at this thing called life.

I heard a story recently about a young Episcopal priest from Philadelphia. This man is about my age, maybe a little older. He is the priest for a large Episcopal church in Downtown Philadelphia. This church is so big it holds three services each Sunday in which the pews are completely packed.

Well this young Episcopal priest had a dream. His dream was to take the cemetery that the church owned and develop it into a school. There was only one grave in this cemetery, it was the grave of John Wanamaker, the pioneer of the first department store which was called John Wanamaker and Co.

The reason this young priest wanted to take this cemetery and build a school was because the school system in Philadelphia was a private system. So, every student had to apply to the various schools around the city which meant that some kids didn't get into the top schools or even the mediocre schools.

It meant that the kids who lived in the impoverished areas and didn't have a well-known last name or lots of money to donate, went to the worst schools and just got lost in the system until they ended up in the streets involved with drugs and committing crimes.

So, this young priest went and talked to everyone he knew in order to have John Wanamaker's grave moved from this cemetery, and this have this cemetery approved for a school to be built on it.

Despite all the work and red tape, he got it done and it was all approved.

Next this young priest had to contact everyone he knew in the church, out of the church, and around the city for donations and investments for this school project.

Despite all the hard work, he secured the funding for the school and over the span of a year and half it was built.

Next this young priest decided that he and some of his friends were going to get on their bikes and ride around the roughest parts of Philadelphia. As they rode around these parts and ran into the kids in the street, he and his friends would talk to the kids who had been denied from all the other schools, and he invited them to come to his school, for free. There were no application fees like the other schools and there were no yearly dues.

The kids that this priest and his friends reached out to an invited, were elated about this new possibility. They enrolled and then they worked hard to stay in that school. They were required to attend school 6 days a week, and the one day they had off they were required to go to church.

After just one year of being in operation, there was a graduating class of 86 kids. There was a graduating class of 86 kids who didn't have much hope for their lives, or their future and they received a high school diploma. 86 kids who would have probably ended up in jail or dead from drug overdose, that were given a new opportunity and a new possibility.

It took a lot of hard work from this young priest and it took a lot of hard work from those kids, but they all put the work in and did something great!

God wants us to dream big. God wants us to look at our lives and this world and see endless possibilities no matter our age and no matter our circumstance.

We know it takes hard work to achieve great things, but God wants us to work hard at making our life and this world a better place.

God wants us to Get up and Walk with Him!

May we all awaken to the possibilities that surround us, and may we put in the hard work that it takes to achieve these things.

In the name of the Father, the Son and the Holy Spirit. Amen.

God is Always with Us
Isaiah 25:6-9; Romans 6:3-9

Our text from Isaiah came as a sudden and surprising interruption to what the Israelites had previously been experiencing.

In the previous chapters of Isaiah, the Israelites had been experiencing upheaval in their land. There was a raging war with Syria. The Assyrians were working to conquer Israel, the northern kingdom, which in turn threatened Judah in the south.

In the previous chapter, Isaiah delineated how the country of Israel had gone amuck. Some of the inhabitants of Israel had broken their covenant with God. They had violated the laws and statues established by God.

In response to all that, Isaiah announces that God is going to destroy the land and destroy all those that were seeking to oppress the faithful. In verse 3 of the previous chapter, Isaiah says,

> *"The earth shall be utterly laid waste and utterly despoiled."*

He goes on to say in verse 6:

> *Therefore, a curse devours the earth and its inhabitants suffer for their guilt; therefore, the inhabitants of the earth dwindled, and few people are left.*

> *The wine dries up the vine languishes all the merry-hearted sigh.*

> *No longer do they drink wine with singing; strong drink is bitter to those who drink it.*

> *The city of chaos is broken down every house is shut up so that no one can enter.*

> *There is an outcry in the streets for lack of wine; all joy has reached its eventide; the gladness of the earth is banished.*

It is quite a stark contrast to what we encountered in our passage from Isaiah before.

In this chapter of Isaiah, there is an announcement of a grand elaborate feast. A feast that nobody expected. A feast that came as a sudden surprise. This elaborate feast was the signal that the Israelites had been hoping for, praying for, and yearning for.

It was the sudden signal that God was, in fact, with them during those difficult and dark years as the war raged on.

It was the sudden signal that the impending crisis they had been experiencing had a silver lining to it—that God was with them and had a plan to restore their lives. It was a foretaste of what was to come with the change and shift in the Israelites situation.

In these few verses, God declares that the shroud of desperation that covered the city "like a veil" would now be lifted. Mount Zion, the mountain top that the whole city of Jerusalem was built upon, would now be liberated from danger and the reputation of the city and the people would now be restored. No longer would they experience pain and distress, and death and destruction.

Instead God would wipe away their tears. He would ease their fears, and he would finally answer their cries of distress.

I heard one bible scholar describe this event in Isaiah this way. She said:

> On this mountain top, God Himself prepares a sumptuous, Julia-Childs-worthy meal. God crawls to the back of the wine cellar and retrieves the best of the vintage wines that have aged for years. On this mountain top, God lays out all the good china and the wine glasses are sparkling. On this mountain, God will not only nurture and feed God's people, but God declares and promises to destroy all evil to destroy "the shroud", "the sheet", the veil that was covering His people. On this mountain, God proclaims He will swallow up death forever.

Turns out this feast on top of Mount Zion is a feast of triumph over death. A celebration, a feast, to praise and honor and thank God for His defeat over evil. A feast to celebrate the new thing God was doing in and amongst the Israelites—a new life and a new way of life He was generating for the Israelites.

It's a very beautiful image. It's a heartwarming depiction of the God we know, love, and trust. It depicts a God who swoops in during our darkest, most painful times, and wipes our tears, eases our fears, and finally answers our cries of distress. It is a stunning articulation of hope that we find here in this passage of Isaiah, but we know that is not the full picture.

We know that the war continued to rage on in Israel for several more years. We know that eventually the Israelites were marched off to exile where they lived in captivity for many years.

So how do we read this passage and interpret these hope-filled words that Isaiah shares when we know what is still yet to come?

How do we read these words and interpret them when we know that death and calamity was still a reality for the Israelites?

In turn, how are we to understand this so called, "defeat over death and evil" when we ourselves still experience death's sting in our own personal lives?

How are we to affirm that the God we love and serve is a God that has in fact swallowed up death and removed the veil of evil when the first thing we see when we turn on our television are things like the shooting that occurred in Pittsburg—in a synagogue of all places. A place that is holy and sacred, a place that is certainly believed to be occupied by God.

How are we to share a message of how God has defeated evil and death when we so commonly hear stories about school shootings, one of which most recently occurred in the suburbs of Charlotte just this past week.

All week long my Facebook news feed has been filled with comments and questions from clergy friends and colleagues regarding both of these events. The most reoccurring statement and question made by them is, "How long, O Lord? How long, O Lord before you hear our cries before you answer our prayers for mercy? How long before you finally answer our cries of distress?"

These are real life questions that we all wrestle with. We all wrestle with the notion of theodicy, the existence of evil that pervades our world and what God's role is in that.

We all wrestle with why we have such tragic events that occur in our world and question why God doesn't swoop in and prevent such evil from pervading our communities. Or why an all-powerful, all knowing, all loving God could allow such atrocities to continually occur.

And I don't know that we, as Christians, can truly and honestly ever really answer that question. I don't know that anyone possesses a definitive answer or explanation as to why such evil exists.

Limited human perception theory is a theory that states, as humans our finite thinking, our limited scope of understanding, doesn't allow us to fully understand and comprehend why evil exists.

As humans, we cannot see the big picture, so we are not able to conceptualize how or why death and evil play a part in our lives. This theory makes the argument that from our limited human viewpoint, we cannot see the broad picture, whereas God is beyond time, able to suspend time, and can see the past, the present, and the future. Therefore, Only God can weave it all together and make sense of it.

Now we may wish we had all the answers. We may wish we knew why evil exists and how God plays a role in it all. We may wish for quick and easy solutions to our significant problems and needs, but we know that answers and quick and easy resolutions to the crises and the problems we face is not always possible.

And if we tried to resolve every person's crisis and every nations calamity with our limited understanding and our finite minds, then we would experience the same type of chaos that Jim Carrey observed when he granted every human's prayer request in *Bruce Almighty*.

In that humorous movie, Bruce, or Jim Carey, has taken on the role of God and he has been inundated with prayer requests. So, Jim Carey tries several ways to organize the prayers, so he can handle them and respond to them. He finally organizes them in the form of e-mails, but after spending all night trying to answer prayers at rapid speed, he realizes that there are more prayers than he can possibly handle, so he decides to reply yes to all of them.

Suddenly chaos is occurring around the world. Thousands of people win the lottery at once (which means the payout-per-person is very small) which eventually results in a riot, and Bruce can't figure out why everyone's upset. That is just one example of the chaos that erupted as a result of answering YES to everyone's prayer requests, but it's a great depiction of how there are no easy answers and no easy fixes in life.

It's a great depiction of limited human perception theory—how our finite minds are not able to conceptualize how this whole thing called life works. We are not equipped. Only God knows and only God is equipped to handle and respond to it and weave it all together.

Going back to the shooting in Pittsburgh last week. There were vigils all around our nation in response to that horrific shooting. There was even a vigil in Asheville where 200 people showed up.

As people all around our nation gathered together to grieve and mourn with one another, I pondered what words of hope could really help them. What you would you say to those individuals who are heartbroken, scared, and left feeling hopeless, and feel like our world is full of hate?

Considering that event, I pondered our passage from Isaiah and how we could truly proclaim Isaiah's message found in this passage when you know what is still yet to come?

How do you proclaim a message that God has removed the veil of evil and swallowed up death forever when you know there is going to be another shooting and another tragedy? That is just the sad reality of the world that we live in.

As I pondered this timely topic earlier this week, I spoke with a good friend of mine, Christopher Tweel. Christopher serves as pastor of a church in Richmond, Virginia, and at one point he lived in Pittsburgh right down the street from where the shooting in the synagogue took place.

As I spoke with him, he told me what the rabbi had said during the vigil that occurred in Richmond. At that vigil about several hundred people were present, and as the Rabbi offered his words in response to what had occurred in Pittsburgh he said:

> I am aware of how all this makes us feel. As a community of God's people, we feel lost, afraid, vulnerable, and hurt. But as a community of God's people, we must refuse to face life with despair. As a community of God's people, we must face life with hope and with a deep care for one another. That is the path forward for us.

So how do you proclaim a message of how God has removed the evil veil and sting of death in our present day and age?

You remind folks that despite the evil that exists in this world, and even though evil will continue to exist in its many and various forms, God is still with us during it all.

That despite the many tragic events that occur daily, God is with us to wipe our tears, to ease our fears, and to soothe our cries of distress. God is with us and has a plan to vindicate, and liberate, and restore our lives in His own timing and on His own terms.

God's ways are mysterious, and we may not be able to comprehend why terrible things happen, but what we do know is that God always has an overarching plan.

Our text from Isaiah invites us to wait patiently for the time, for the moment, for the sudden signal when God will in fact remove the shroud of darkness that covers the land when tragedy strikes.

Isaiah asks us to wait patiently for the sudden and unexpected signal when God will swallow up the sting of death and create a grand elaborate feast for his people, even if it does only last for one chapter.

Ultimately, this passage asks us to wait patiently, as we know and trust that no matter what we face in life, no matter if there are years of war ahead of us, followed by years of captivity, to know and trust that God is always with us, and there will come a feast once again.

In the name of the Father, the Son, and the Holy Spirit. Amen.

Honoring the Divine
Matthew 22:34-46

In this passage, Matthew begins with a question. It began with the Pharisees asking Jesus which of the commandments is the greatest?

When the Pharisees asked this question, they weren't asking a straight forward question. It was a loaded question. It was a question full of hidden landmines. Essentially, they were asking Jesus to choose one of God's commandments that was the greatest, however if He picked just one, then He would be emphasizing His favorites whilst ignoring the others. Then the Pharisees could fire back with accusations, saying Jesus was a heretic.

They could then accuse Jesus of being a heretic, because according to the Pharisees every commandment of the law is great, and all the commandments come from God, therefore, it is God's will to obey each one of His commandments.

On the other hand, if Jesus was to answer the way they would have liked for Him to, saying, "all the commandments of God are important because they come from God, and it is God's will that we obey each one of His laws", then the Pharisees could fire back with a barrage of accusations of how He had broken numerous laws and commandments.

They could follow up by asking if He would please tell they why He was doing work on the Sabbath, or why He was teaching people to disregard the strict dietary codes. They could fire back saying, "Why are you not eating according to God's law or following the cleanliness code, which required them to wash their hands before each meal and avoid contact with blood?

So, this question was loaded and confrontational to say the least. It was most certainly a catch 22, and Jesus knew that, which is why he framed His answer the way He did. Jesus answered it in such a way that avoided all those hidden landmines.

He answered by saying, "You shall love the Lord your God with all your heart, and with all your soul, and with all your mind. This is the greatest and first commandment. And the second is like it: "You shall love your neighbor as yourself."

And before one of the Pharisees could interject with any questions or accusations, Jesus said, "On these two commandments hang all the law and the prophets."

The last part is the most important. That last part when Jesus said, "On these two commandments hangs all the laws and the prophets", that is what got Him out of this catch 22. When Jesus said, "On these two commandments hangs all the law and prophets," he wasn't denouncing any of the old codes and laws, thereby making Himself out to be a heretic. He wasn't incriminating himself or painting Himself to be a law-breaking heathen.

Instead, He framed His answer in such a way where all the prior laws and Old Testament codes were still relevant and valid. He framed it in such a way where the laws of old had been swallowed up by these two broad sweeping commandments.

It was on these two commandments that all the others hinged. In fact, on these two commandments hinges the entire Bible.

There are 613 Old Testament laws and codes. So, when Jesus responded this way, He took the words of all 613 commandments of the Law and cut straight to the chase. He cut straight to the chase about God's will; He cut straight to the core of God's purpose—which is to love God, and to love your neighbor as yourself.

That brings us to the larger over-arching question of this passage and that is: What does it really mean to love the Lord your God with all your heart, with all your soul, and with all your mind? What does that look like? How do we do that? How do we really love our neighbor as yourself?

In Hinduism, there is a tradition where those practicing Hinduism in an area, neighborhood, town or village, they all go around late at night and leave offerings for their neighbors. They will go around late at night and place flowers on people's doorsteps. They go around and leave food at their neighbor's stoop. They will spend a couple hours creating these beautiful elaborate drawings in chalk in front of their neighbor's door stoop, and they leave lit candles out there for so when their neighbors wake up in the morning and step outside, they encounter all these wonderful and beautiful things that were left for them out of love and appreciation. It's a beautiful Hindu ritual and an example of one way in which they love and honor their neighbor. It is how they show their love and appreciation to their neighbor

It is also very similar to how they show love and appreciation to the various gods of their faith tradition. They show their love to a specific god by lighting candles, making offerings with food and incense. So, through this ritualistic practice of making these offerings late at night on their neighbors' doorsteps, what they really are doing is taking time to recognize the divine spirit in their neighbor. Taking the time to honor and respect the divine spirit that resides in each of their neighbors, and then leaving an offering to salute that divine spirit in each of them.

In addition to this practice, there is a Hindu Sanskrit word that is commonly used which is, *namaste*. In places where Hinduism is practiced, this word is commonly used throughout their day-to-day interactions. *Namaste*, translates as "the divine in me recognizes and honors the divine in you."

Simply put *namaste* refers to a person *waking up* to the divine spirit of another and taking a moment to recognize the divine spirit that runs through all of us, the divine spirit that connects us all in sacred and indisputable ways.

So, when people use this term, *Namaste*, essentially what they are saying to one another is:

- My divine spirit bows to your divine spirit.

- I salute all that is divine within you.

- The spirit in me honors the spirit in you.

- The light in me honors the light in you.

I think that this Hindu practice of leaving offerings on your neighbors' doorsteps and the use of this word *namaste* throughout a person's day-to-day interactions, answer those two questions I posed earlier. These two practices serve to address how we really can love the Lord our God with all our heart, with all our mind, with all our soul

It depicts what it means or looks like to love God with every ounce of our being and to love your neighbor as yourself. It answers those questions because in order to fulfill those two commandments, it means we must look for the divine in other people. It means we take the time to search out the divine spirit in each person whom we meet, and we bow to that spirit, we salute and honor that spirit, and we make a love offering to that spirit.

A great Norwegian novelist, John Bojer, had another take on this idea about how to love God and neighbor. He writes about how we can fulfill these two commandments in his story titled, *The Great Hunger*.

The story starts by describing a newcomer that had moved into a village. This newcomer was not social. He liked to keep to himself. He was reclusive and had no interest in building relationships with other people.

So, when this anti-social newcomer moved into the village, he put a fence up all around his property, and then he posted a sign on this fence surrounding his property which read, **"Keep Out."** He then put a vicious dog within the confines of the fence to keep anyone from climbing over it and coming and knocking on his door.

One day the neighbor's little girl reached her arm inside this man's fence because she wanted to pet the dog. When she did, the dog latched his jaws onto her arm and savagely bit it off.

As you might imagine the daughter's father was furious, and the townspeople were enraged, and this man was shunned from the community and everyone refused to speak to him.

The owners of the local grocery store wouldn't sell him groceries anymore. When it came time to start planting seeds for the garden, the owners of the seed store wouldn't sell him seed. It eventually got to the point where the man became destitute, and he didn't know what to do in order to survive.

One day this man looked out his window, and he saw another man out in his field sowing seed on his field. He ran out and discovered it was the father of the little girl. "Why are you doing this for me? Everyone in this town has shunned me and you of all people have every right to hate me!"

The father replied, "I am doing this to keep God alive in me."

It is a profound story that Boer writes. Profound in so much that it reflects the struggles that we all face. The struggle we face with forgiving people, the struggle we face with letting go of anger, resentment, or bitterness. It highlights the struggle we face with rising above anything that our neighbor(s) may have done to us and choosing to love them despite it all.

Rising above whatever may have occurred in the past and choosing to still see the divine in them. Going a step further, choosing to look for ways in which we can honor that divine spirit and make an offering to that spirit.

The man in Bojer's story could have clung to the hatred and resentment and bitterness he felt towards his neighbor because of what happened to his daughter. He had every reason to, right?

But instead, he chose to rise above it all. He chose to search out and find the divine spirit that resided in his neighbor. He sought out ways in which he could honor that spirit and then he made an offering to that man by planting seed in his field and helping him to survive.

Much like the practices of Hinduism that I mentioned and much like Bojer's story, as God's children, we are called to love one other. We are called to look for ways in which we really can love God and neighbor.

We are called to look for ways in which we can really honor the divine spirit in each one of our neighbors and salute the divine.

When we are able to do that, that is when we fulfill those two commandments on which the whole entire bible hinges. Moreover, that is how we keep God alive in us all.

In the name of the Father, the Son, and the Holy Spirit. Amen.

Reconnect and Recharge
Mark 6:30-34; 53-56

Prior to moving to Weaverville, NC I was living in Western NY. I was living in the small snowy village of Westfield, New York. Immediately when I moved there I noticed how active that community was. Everyone was constantly outside doing something. People were out walking the dog, biking, downhill skiing, cross country skiing, snowmobiling, gardening, farming, or shoveling. It did not matter what season of the year it was, people were always out and about doing something.

I remember within the first couple of months living there, I had plans to meet a girlfriend for dinner. On that day, we had gotten a lot of snow—about 6 inches or so. That amount was nothing in comparison to what all the locals were used to getting. However, on that day, I kept waiting to get a text message or a phone call from my friend saying that we needed to cancel our dinner plans, since it was snowing out and the roads were covered in snow.

But that never happened, and much to my surprise, my friend showed up at my doorstep to pick me up, and we proceeded with our dinner plans.

When you live in the south if there is even one snow flake in the sky, businesses shut down, schools close for the day sometimes even for the week. Everyone makes a mad dash to the grocery store to pick up bread and milk and anything else you made need. All plans that you had scheduled for that day come to a screeching halt.

That is not so much the case up there in Western New York. Nothing stops, regardless of how many feet of snow you get. Life continues, and nothing interrupts your daily activities.

So, as I found myself living in a community that was always burning the candles at both ends and often times torching the candle at both ends, I fell into that pattern of living as well. As I fell into that pattern of living and became aware of all the "busyness" then it caused me to hear Jesus' message in this passage in a new light. I came to understand Jesus' invitation from our passage in Mark this morning in a new and different way.

It shed a whole new light on what Jesus was trying to get the disciples to do, and what He was trying to help them to understand.

In this passage of Mark, we encountered Jesus and His disciples returning from a stint of traveling. They had been teaching and proclaiming the good news, and as they returned from their travels Jesus offered them an invitation. He told them, "Come away with me to a quiet deserted place and rest for a while."

When Jesus said this, He was trying to get the disciples to realize the importance of retreating, the importance of going off to a quiet deserted place, to slow down, and to take a break from life's "busyness". Jesus was trying to illustrate the importance of sitting and being still for a while.

In our own day-to-day lives, it is not very often that we slow down and take a rest, or retreat to a quiet deserted place. It is not very often that we take time to sit and be still. If we do decide to take a break from our daily activities, instead of crossing off another item on our to do list, then we feel like we are lazy. We feel like we are wasting the day away, not accomplishing anything, and not being productive.

Think about how many times someone asks you how your day was, and you respond with a long list of things that you accomplished that day. We respond to that question by saying things like, "Oh, it was a great day. I mowed the lawn, went grocery shopping, did 17 loads of laundry, washed the car, and bathed the dog. It was a good and productive day!"

We would never answer that question by saying, "Oh, it was such a great and productive day. I did absolutely nothing!"

As Americans, it is easy for us to get caught up in this mode of constantly doing. Constantly working, and constantly accomplishing something. So, Jesus' invitation, to "Come away with Him to a quiet deserted place and rest for a while," is an invitation for us to loosen our shackles and climb out of the cages that we have constructed from this culturally-fed belief that we must always be doing something.

It is an invitation to dismiss this notion and belief that we must be doing something, in order to be deemed a productive member of society.

The point Jesus was trying to make here was to show the disciples, and us, how doing nothing and being still can be one of the most beneficial and productive things we can do for ourselves at times.

Bill Hybels is a gifted preacher and pastor at a church in Chicago, and in one closing session of a conference he keynoted, he described a simple practice that had completely transformed his church.

He told of some years ago when he encountered a young man after a Sunday service who asked very directly, "Pastor could you tell me how I can connect with God?"

Hybels reached for the simplest response he could think of and said, "Well, the first thing you need to do is set aside some time every day to be with God."

When the young man protested that he was too busy for that the pastor responded gently by pointing out how when something really matters in life, then one manages to make time for it.

Then he made this suggestion. He said, "Go home and pick out the most comfortable chair in your house and arrange it in your favorite space in your house. Whether near the window, or somewhere in a dimmer lit space." The Pastor then told the man to decide on a particular time each day that he could go to that chair so that he could sit for a while. Whether early morning or late in the afternoon or just before bed.

The Pastor told the man to plan on sitting in that quiet space for 30 minutes or so.

Then he said, and during that time read a passage from scripture—one of the gospels, or a psalm, or some other spiritual reading. And then just sit with it.

During that time the pastor told the man to ask himself what that passage might be saying to him. He said, "Think about your day and the challenges you're facing, and ask God for guidance, wisdom and strength. Then close with a prayer."

The pastor concluded by saying the key though, is to go to your chair regularly every day if possible.

The young man was so inspired by his pastor's proposal that he went out and purchased a new oak rocking chair and put it by the fireplace in his home. Pastor Hybels says it changed that man's entire life.

For more than 25 years after that, this man went to his chair virtually every day. In doing so, he found a new grounding, a new lively faith that shaped all the major decisions in his life from that point on.

That simple idea caught on in that church in a big way, and a great theme and motto for that congregation emerged where everyone began asking the question, "Where is your chair?"

One of the best and most beneficial things we can do for ourselves is to take some time to rest, so that we can reconnect with God and begin to feed life back into our spiritual lives again.

When we are constantly going and doing, we get caught up in ourselves, we get caught up in our own personal pursuits, and our daily activities. Our focus and attention are more on the task at hand, rather than on our relationship with God, and the tasks God would have us accomplish.

The practice of Sabbath, the practice of taking a rest from life's activities, is our opportunity to encounter God in a palpable way and to reconnect with Him.

I was at a conference recently and a speaker talked about an experience that he had at Montreat Conference Center once. He said that while he was visiting Montreat one year, Lake Susan was being drained because they had to fix the water fountain in the middle of the lake. So, since Lake Susan had temporarily been turned into Crater Susan, it had forced him to go and find a different place to sit and relax.

As he settled into his spot, he looked around, and all he could see were mountains. The beautiful Blue Ridge Mountains were completely surrounding him. He remembered how he had once heard someone describe the Blue Ridge Mountains as God's way of hugging us, God's way of wrapping His arms around us and cradling us.

He said as he sat there with the Blue Ridge Mountains cradling him and God hugging him, he said he felt as if he was resting in the curve of God's smile.

As Children of God, it is important for us to take time to rest in the curve of God's smile from time to time. It is so important for us to be still for a while so that we can reconnect with God.

For it is in those moments, when we are resting in the curve of God's smile that we can step away from all the other things that usually drive and consume us. It affords us the opportunity to sense and detect God's presence in our lives once more.

Howard Thurman in a message entitled, "The Genuine in You" said, and I am paraphrasing:

Failing to listen to the sound of the genuine in us, is to render ourselves always on the ends of strings being pulled by something or someone else. Taking the time to be still and know, refreshes us to remember both who we are and whose we are.

In addition to that, there is one other reason why resting is one of the most beneficial and productive things we can do for ourselves, and that is that it allows us to recharge.

It allows us to take the time we need in order to recharge so that we can do God's work in this world and further the kingdom of God.

Our passage from Mark this morning began with the disciples returning from a long stint of traveling around ministering, preaching, teaching, and sharing the good news with others. It also ended with Jesus and the disciples healing the sick.

So, this passage is book ended with Jesus and the disciples doing ministry and furthering the kingdom of God. In between those two bookends, we hear Jesus saying to the disciples, "Take a break. Retreat for a minute and sit down and rest for a while."

Essentially, Jesus was illustrating how retreating and resting for a while is imperative for having an effective ministry or for being able to do ministry at all.

It teaches us that if we do not retreat to reconnect *with* God then we will have nothing left to give *to* God.

I heard a story recently about two men. One man challenged another man to an all-day wood chopping contest. The challenger worked very hard stopping only for a brief lunch break.

The other man had a leisurely lunch and took several breaks during the day. At the end of the day the challenger was surprised and annoyed to find that the other fellow had chopped substantially more wood than he had.

"I don't get it" he said. "Every time I checked you were taking a rest, yet you chopped more wood than I did."

The other man replied, "But you didn't notice that I was sharpening my ax when I sat down to rest!"

We are all doing ministry. It is not just the ministers or team leaders. We are all helping to care for others. We all give of ourselves to other people in many various ways. In order to do that effectively, we must take a rest.

It is in those times of rest that we allow ourselves to be sharpened and we regain our strength. We cannot constantly give of ourselves, without feeding something back into ourselves. Output requires input and intake. Work calls for rest.

Ben Campbell Johnson a Presbyterian Minister and professor at Columbia Theological Seminary once stated:

"Perhaps you need to consider a retreat because you were made for both engagement and withdrawal. Engagement with the world and life and withdrawal to be renewed and re-created. In the Creation story this profound truth is modeled in the action of God who labored for six days and rested on the seventh. Johnson says, "What kind of Superman or Wonder Woman would it take to say, 'God may need a day to withdrawal and rest, but I don't!'"

Withdrawal and rest are vitally important, not only for our own spiritual wellbeing, but for the spiritual wellbeing of others. When we take a break from all the other events and activities that fill our days, it allows us to reconnect with God, and it allows us to recharge so we can carry on with the work of God.

We may live in a world that constantly feeds this idea and notion that productivity means we must constantly be doing and accomplishing something and scratching another thing off our to-do list.

But there is most certainly something valuable and productive that comes from resting in the curve of God's smile and retreating with our Lord.

May we all leave from here this morning with a renewed insight about Jesus' invitation to retreat to a quiet deserted place and may we take him up on that offer.

May we start to gravitate away from this notion that we must constantly be doing something in order to be productive in this world. Instead may we re-define our concept of productivity to include times of resting and retreating with our Lord.

In the name of the Father the Son and the Holy Spirit. Amen.

Stewardship: Investing in God
Matthew 25:14-30

It is important to reflect on what it means and looks like to be God's good stewards of all that he has entrusted us with. As we take a few minutes to ponder that idea and notion, I would like for you to recall the third character in the parable from Matthew.

The third character in this parable had taken what his master had given him, the talents he had been entrusted with, and out of fear he buried them.

As we keep this third character's actions in mind, I wanted to share a story with you from my travels a few weeks ago.

As you know I traveled to Portugal and Spain to hike the Camino, I flew over to Morocco for 5 days. While I was there, I stayed with a friend named Rebecca. Rebecca and I traveled to Assilyah.

Assylah is a small walled city and ancient city with all kinds of murals all over the walls. So, we walked around Assylah for a little while, grabbed lunch, then we headed back to the train station, so we could catch the train to Fez where Rebecca lives.

Fez is about a 5-hour train ride, and there are only a few trains that go that direction a day. So, we grabbed our luggage and started walking to the train station. The train station was about a mile and half walk which should only take about 25 minutes or so.

As we started walking, I had my hiking pack on my back, which weighed 20lbs or so. I had been used to carrying it for weeks at that point, so it wasn't a problem and Rebecca had a suit case with wheels that she was pulling.

Well, one of the wheels on her suitcase was broken. It was completely flat, so Rebecca was basically just dragging this suitcase down the sidewalk which was slowing us down quite a bit.

I noticed the train departure time was nearing, so I offered to help drag her suitcase. I would drag for a little bit, then get tired, and then she would drag it for a bit. So, we traded on and off like this for quite some time.

As the time pressed on it didn't seem like we are putting much of a dent in that mile and half walk to the train station, and the departure times was getting closer and closer. So, Rebecca looked at me and said we are going to need to get a taxi or we will never make it and we'll be stuck in Assilyah overnight. So, I said, "Sure, let's get a taxi. No problem." In fact, there was a problem, because there were no taxis.

Assylah isn't a high tourist area so there weren't tons of taxis or even tons of people around for that matter. So, then Rebecca says "We are going to have to flag a car down and ask someone to take us to the train station. Before I could even process what she had said, that we were going to be hitchhiking, she was out in the street flagging down the first car she saw.

The car stopped. She said in Arabic, *train station*. He in Arabic says, "Yes, get in." Rebecca opens the door to the backseat and then looks at me and says get in. To which I replied, "No way. I am not getting in that vehicle."

Every possible scenario of things that could go wrong went through my mind in that moment. Every warning from my father went through my head, and there was no way I was getting in that vehicle.

Well when I looked Rebecca in the eyes and said there's no way, I'm getting in that car. I could see the fury in her eyes. I could see the realization setting in that we were going to have to keep dragging that luggage down the street and more than likely miss our train.

When I saw that fury, I said, "Okay I'm getting that vehicle and so I climbed in."

Clearly everything went alright because I am standing here today telling you the story. Our driver was very nice. He drove us right to the train station, and we made the train on time.

During the train ride, Rebecca explained a little bit of the Moroccan culture to me. She said the Moroccan culture believes that if one has been blessed with something, then they are to offer it to others. They are to share what they have been given from God.

She went on to say, for the most part, Moroccans think Americans are materialistic and that we are hoarders. We hoard what we have been blessed with instead of openly and freely sharing it with all others even strangers.

For the Moroccans, if someone has been blessed with a vehicle then of course they will share it with others. They will offer a ride to someone with no questions asked. They will lend their vehicle to someone who may need it for the day. They believe they have been blessed and so they want to offer God's blessings to others.

For us we would never do. We are fearful about what might happen. We are fearful that if we lend our car to someone then that person could end up wrecking it and our insurance would go up or we could get sued. Or we think if we stop and pick up a stranger then bad things could happen.

These may be very logical and rational fears, but for the Moroccans, their way of life entails living outside the bounds of those fears. It entails offering whatever they have, what they have been entrusted with, whatever they have been blessed with, to all others.

Much like we find in our parable with that third character, it is sometimes fear that prevents us (Americans) from being able to fully embrace the Moroccan way of thinking.

It is sometimes fear that prevents us from being able to receive or experience the gifts and talents of others. It is sometimes fear that prevents us from taking risks and offering our talents and investing our gifts in other people and Gods kingdom. It is fear that keeps a lot of us just as bound as that third character in our parable.

Let me share a story with you about what happens when we operate outside of the bounds of fear.

Several months ago, I started reading a very interesting book. It is called, The *Hidden Life of Trees*. It is about a German scientist by the name of Peter Wohlen.

Peter manages the forest in the Eifel mountains in Germany. He spent quite some time researching and studying the trees of that forest, most of which are Beech trees.

Once I found out his book was mostly about Beech trees, I was even more intrigued because of where we live surrounded by these beautiful large Beech trees here in the Beech Community.

In his book he writes about how the forest is a social network. These Beech trees live in community with one another.

He makes the case that Beech trees are like humans; they huddle together in community with one another, communicating with each other, supporting one another so they can grow tall and wide.

They share nutrients with each other paying special attention to the trees that may be sick and sending more sugar and nutrients to those members, so they get better.

These Beech trees even go as far as warning each other when there is an impending threat or danger; when there is a predator near. And they do so by releasing a certain scent in the air that the other Beech trees can smell and pick up on.

Once the other trees smell this scent, they release toxins into their branches and leaves so if/when a predator bites their leaves, they'll die, and it wards off future predators.

It's a super fascinating book. The author goes into detail to explain how these trees are connected and why they stay connected and huddled together in communities like this.

In this book he states a trees most important means to staying connected to other trees is something he calls a "wood-wide web".

A "wood-wide web" of soil and fungi that connects vegetation in an intimate network and allows the sharing of an enormous amount of information and goods.

Peter describes, in his book, how there really does exist an interdependence amongst the tree colonies and how most individual trees of the same species grow in the same stand and are connected to each other through their root system.

So below the earth's surface is this "wood-wide web" of interconnectedness where roots overlap, and connect, and feed sugar, and nutrients to one another.

He goes on to say it appears that nutrient exchange and helping neighbors in times of need is the rule. That is what ensures their life and longevity. If every tree were looking out only for itself then quite a few of them would never reach old age.

Regular fatalities would result in many large gaps in the tree canopy which would make it easier for storms to get inside the forest and uproot more trees.

The heat of summer would reach the forest floor and dry it out. *Every tree would suffer.*

Therefore, every tree is valuable to the community and plays an intricate role in working to keep all the trees in that community around for as long as possible.

Super fascinating, right?

These are just a couple of the excerpts that I wanted to share with you from this book. Both of which speak to us as members of the Beech community, and more specifically they speak to us as we are amidst our stewardship season.

In the first excerpt Peter writes:

Whoever has an abundance of sugar hands some over. Whoever is running short gets help. They work together to ensure that each individual member of that immediate community and huddle of trees is getting what it needs to survive.

Therefore, a tree can only be as strong as the forest, the huddle that surrounds it. A tree's wellbeing depends on their community.

He goes on to say, essentially that is the age old saying: a chain is only as strong as its weakest link. Trees could have come up with that saying because they know this intuitively, and they do not hesitate to help each other out.

To tie it to our New Testament lesson, they are not fearful of giving away what they have or investing it in others. They are not afraid to invest what they have been given, back into their neighbor and offer some of their own sugar and nutrients, because they know that if they give what they have, it keeps their community alive. Thereby ensuring their own longevity.

Much like the Beech tree, this church depends on its community. It depends on each and every single one of its members for its survival. It takes all of us working together and contributing what we have: our time, our talents, and our resources, to keep our church community alive. Thereby ensuring our own longevity here in this valley.

As our parable pointed out, there are two ways we can go through life. We can go through life scared and afraid of investing what we have, fearful that we may run out of resources, fearful that it may affect us negatively, fearful of taking the risk. Perhaps even hoarding what we possess, instead of investing it back in God's people and God's kingdom.

Or, we can go through life offering what we do have. Investing what we have been given back in other people. Taking what we have so generously been blessed with, and investing it back in our church, back in our community, and back in God's kingdom. Investing what we have been blessed with, so that our church, this community, and God's kingdom here on earth can continue to exist and grow strong.

As Peter Wohlen pointed out in his book, these Beech trees are symbols of community as they huddle together, leaning on another, making sure each member has what it needs to survive. Leaning on one other so their community can continue to thrive and exist.

When we operate outside the bounds of fear, it ensures the life and longevity of this church and our community.

May we all operate outside of the bounds of fear. Taking what we have, what we have been entrusted with, and investing it back into this church, back into our community, and back into God's kingdom.

In the name of the Father, the Son, and the Holy Spirit. Amen.

A Willingness to Serve
1 Kings 17: 8-16

Destitution and desperation are two words that immediately come to mind when we read our Old Testament passage this morning from 1 Kings chapter 17.

The poor widow in this passage has no food and is on the brink of starvation. This passage carries strong images of poverty, destitution, and desperation in the face of what seems like a pretty bleak and hopeless situation.

To make matters worse, we know this poor widow had already faced some hard and tragic times. We know that her husband died prematurely, leaving her to raise their child in a day and age when it was quite difficult for a woman to fend for herself.

So, with the death of her husband and considering this passage, we know that death, tragedy, difficult times, and desperation have played a primary role throughout this woman's life.

The other character in this story, Elijah, is no stranger to desperate and destitute times either.

At the time 1 Kings was written, King Ahab was the King, and he had issued a decree stating that all prophets of the Lord were to be found and put to death.

So, Elijah had gone into hiding. He had been living in exile and was fleeing place to place fearful for his life.

That is when God told him to go to Zarephath where he would encounter this widow that God would help take care of him. This widow would provide him with food and water.

When God told Elijah to flee to Zarephath, Elijah was quite puzzled by this instruction. Elijah knew that that region had been experiencing a severe drought, which in turn had created a long stint of famine.

But instead of rejecting what God was calling him to do, Elijah listened and followed God's instruction. When Elijah arrived on the scene at this widow's home, he not only encountered drought and famine in a big way, but he encountered a woman and her son who were on the brink of starvation.

The widow disclosed that she was gathering sticks to make a fire, so she could make one last little cake of food for her and her son to share, as they prepared themselves for death.

At that point, Elijah tells this widow to not be afraid; To go and do what he says to make a little cake and to bring it to him. And then to make something for herself and her son.

He then says, "For thus says the Lord the God of Israel: The jar of meal will not be emptied, and the jug of oil will not fail until the day that the Lord sends rain on the earth."

And the widow responds by going and doing exactly what Elijah had instructed. She took what little she had left, and she went and made a meal for her and her son, and for Elijah to share.

Call me crazy, but I don't think that we would have responded quite the same way that this poor widow did. For most of us we would have taken what little we had left, and we would have kept it for ourselves. We would have shooed that stranger right off our property and went back into the house to cook our last meal.

I think we can all agree that the actions demonstrated by this widow seem counterintuitive. And what we see happen after that is a miracle story.

What we see happen after that is that God responds by taking what the widow had left and multiplies it.

God responded by filling the widow's flour jar full of all the flour she needed, and then fills the oil jar full of an endless supply of oil. It was enough food and oil to see her through the drought until the rains came again.

It is a wonderful depiction of how our God does indeed perform miracles on our behalf. It is a wonderful depiction of how the God that we love and serve takes care of us, provides for us, and gives us exactly what we need at the very moment that we need it.

It's a great illustration of how God is the ultimate provider of all things we possess in life—the food we eat, the water we drink, all the way down to the very pulse of life. It also depicts what it takes on our behalf to be God's faithful people.

To be God's faithful people means we must be willing to serve the Lord at all costs. It entails taking all that God has given us and entrusted us with and using those things to do God's work.

In order to serve the Lord, we must be willing to let go of any preconceived notions of how we are to spend or use what it is that God has given us and bestowed upon us.

In order to be God's faithful people, we must possess an unwavering willingness to serve the Lord that supersedes doubts, fears, and worries about what it is that God is calling us to do.

The widow in this passage most certainly demonstrated all those things.

The widow was willing to let go of her preconceived notions of how she was to spend and use with what God had entrusted her. The very last of her meal and oil.

She possessed a deep commitment to serve God which superseded her doubts, fears, and worries about how she and her son would survive if they did take what little they had left and fed this stranger at their doorstep.

It was most certainly an act of faith on her part, but it also depicts an unwavering willingness to serve the Lord at all costs.

Recently, I watched a movie called Burnt. It's a movie starring Bradley Cooper who is a chef in a very nice restaurant. It's a Michelin star restaurant, which is a ranking system where restaurants are rewarded 1-3 stars.

So, Bradly Cooper in this movie is the head chef at one of these restaurants that has received the Michelin Star.

As head chef at one of these restaurants, he is known all over the world for his exceptional culinary skills. He eventually gets a little in over his head as his ego takes over and there's a lot of drinking and partying and drug use until that lifestyle eventually leads him to get fired from this high-end restaurant.

So, the rest of the movie is Bradley Cooper trying to get his life back together and wanting to get back to the top of the restaurant game again. He goes to rehab—no more drinking or drugging, he continues reading and studying the leading culinary techniques.

He then approaches a prestigious restaurant owner and pleads to take over his kitchen. To be his head chef with the anticipation and promise of making it a Michelin star restaurant by a certain date.

The restaurant owner agrees, so Bradly Cooper starts traveling all over the world, trying to put together the best possible kitchen team. He goes to Paris, Rome, and London, and all around the world hand-picking the best chefs.

The most interesting clip in this whole movie is when Bradly Cooper is standing in front of one of the chefs that he has tracked down. He is about to ask this young man to leave his current job and move to the states, so he can come work in his kitchen.

As Bradley Cooper stands in front of this guy, the young man is flabbergasted that this great chef is standing before him.

Before Bradley Cooper even starts the whole spiel about coming to work for him, the young man starts singing his praises.

He is going on and on about how great of a chef Cooper is and how he had transformed the whole landscape of the food industry with his knowledge and skills.

At one point the young man says, "You have always been a hero of mine. I have studied your technique and recipes for years."

Bradley Cooper cuts the young man off and he says, "A hero or a God?"

The young man says, "I don't believe I know the difference."

Bradley Cooper says, "Would you come work for me for nothing?"

The young man says, "For nothing?" as if a little shocked.

Bradley Cooper says, "Yea. For nothing. Food and meals, maybe, but for no pay."

Cooper then says, would you pay me to come work for me?"

The young man laughs, and Cooper says, "Would you pay me 100 pounds a week? 200 pounds to come and work under me? What about 300 pounds to come and work for me and to learn from me?"

The young man just stood there stunned by the whole experience.

It was an interesting clip that stuck with me. I thought it was a pretty interesting depiction of what working for God looks like and entails.

Working for God, being faithful followers of God, entails using our time, our talents, and our resources to serve the Lord without expecting any sort of compensation.

It entails paying God really.

Paying God with our tithes each week, paying God by giving our time away for free, putting our talents to work in order to serve Him more in order to further God's work here on earth.

This movie clips echoes the same message and principal of our passage this morning. Working for God entails service, a deep willingness, to serve the Lord at all costs. Working for God entails a deep willingness to serve the Lord without ever expecting God to reward you in any certain way.

The Lord has given each of us so much. God has entrusted each of us with many gifts and talents. Part of being God's faithful people means and entails taking those gifts and talents and putting them to good use. Taking what we have been so generously given and sharing it with other people furthering God's kingdom.

As you are aware, today is the first Sunday of our stewardship season. Every year during the month of November we take a few weeks to remember and emphasize the fact that we are God's people and stewards of all that God has entrusted us with.

So, for the next three weeks we will take some time to really think about and discuss this concept of stewardship. What does it mean to be God's stewards? What does it look like and entail to be good stewards of all that God has given us?

As we conclude our first Stewardship Season Sunday, let us be mindful of the messages found in this passage, messages that remind us of how God is the ultimate provider, how God provides us with all that we have and possess in life from the very food we eat, to the water we drink, to the very pulse of life.

Let us remember that in response to all that God has so generously given us and entrusted us with, then we are to respond by living and acting as God's faithful people. Living and acting as God's faithful people who possess a deep willingness to serve Him at all costs.

In the name of the Father, the Son and the Holy Spirit. Amen.

Fullness in God
Hebrews 10:19-25 & Psalm 16

For just a few moments I would like each of us to take some time and recall a moment in your life when you were completely satisfied. Recall a moment when you were completely content, satiated, and satisfied in life.

Even if that feeling only lasted for a fleeting moment, even if it only lasted for one hour, or one day, or perhaps only one week. But just take a couple seconds to bring that image to the forefront of your mind.

And as you do recall that moment when you felt so content, so satisfied in life. Then I would like you to think about what exactly it was that made you satisfied at that time?

Was it a relationship that was causing that satisfaction? A new budding relationship, perhaps the day you got married. Was it due the birth of a child or a grandchild?

Or did it have more to do with your job or career? Was it a promotion at work that created that sense of satisfaction? Perhaps a new job a new direction your career was headed in?

Maybe it was just the mere fact that you had taken a walk in the woods, and you were mesmerized by the beauty of God's creation. The babbling creek, the colorful trees, the smell of nature that created this deep sense of satisfaction and contentment.

Does your moment of satisfaction have anything to do with taking time for yourself? Getting away from all the pulls and tugs of life?

Does your satisfaction come from cooking, eating, and enjoying a nice meal?

There are all kinds of ways in which a person may become satisfied in life.

In our Psalm this morning we encountered a song where David is singing and expressing his deep satisfaction in life.

He is expressing a longing to continue to experience this sense of contentment and satisfaction in life.

As the Psalm progresses it unfolds the storyline of how the source of David's satisfaction, his fullness in life, is due to his relationship with God.

As the Psalmist begins to unfold for us how and why his deep satisfaction and fullness is found in God, he begins by declaring how the Almighty God is in control of his life and that he is seeking God for safety and refuge.

Now we know that David was not just an ordinary man, and he didn't experience just ordinary struggles.

We know that David was "A Man After God's Own Heart" who experienced heightened levels of trials, tribulations, and wars and much more.

Yet in this Psalm and through everything David endured, he held on to what was most important to him. He held onto the source of his deep satisfaction in life, his relationship with God.

As verse 1 starts out with this declaration for God to protect him, to keep David safe and then moves into a testimony by the end of that verse.

It moves into a testimony of how David has placed his complete trust in God as the ultimate protector. The safest refuge.

The expression David uses, "For in you I take refuge", is a rich metaphor that some Bible scholars say refers to when David was hiding out for safety when Saul was pursuing him.

Others say it refers to David seeking God's protection in the temple. Nevertheless, what is clear is that David is seeking refuge in the Lord and relying upon God for his safety. Trusting that God would protect him from harm's way.

Verse 2 continues to expand upon this declaration of God being the ultimate refuge.

In verse 2 David says, "You are my Lord." Thereby proclaiming that the Lord is in fact the authority in his life. The one who gives direction and purpose and meaning.

David goes on to state in the second half of verse 2, "and there is no good apart from You."

This line seems to say essentially what David was writing about in Psalm 23 when he wrote, "The Lord is my shepherd. I shall not want."

Both Psalms assert how the Lord is the source of all good things in life. That outside of God, there is nothing more that you would need, want or yearn for.

More specifically that God is the very source of life and all goodness that is bestowed upon us in life. Or to quote C.S. Lewis, "He who has God and everything else has no more than he who has God only."

All goodness in life comes from God and apart from God there is no good.

As the Psalm continues to unfold in verses 5 & 6, we hear David delineate all the ways in which God has been the source of life. The source of all goodness in life over the years.

David says, "The Lord is my chosen portion and my cup. You hold my lot. The boundary lines have fallen for me in pleasant places I has a goodly heritage."

This verse echoes similar passages found in Joshua chapters 13-17. Joshua chapters 13-17 discuss the distribution of land in Israel.

It is referring to and referencing the boundary lines. Or the lots that were distributed amongst the tribes of Israel.

This verse invokes thoughts of the gift of land from God. How it was a provision for all that was necessary in life for a livelihood.

Here in verse 5 & 6 of our Psalm, David has reinterpreted the traditional land inheritance imagery of Joshua to sing of his own experience with God. To sing of his own goodness that he so graciously received from God.

Essentially, what David was saying here was that as God had distributed each portion of the land by lot with boundary lines indicating the heritage of the tribes, so the Psalmist had received only goodness in exceedingly pleasant ways from God.

The Psalmist concludes his song with a beautiful statement of how the Lord has shown him the way. The Lord has shown him the path of life.

He is testifying to the fact that the path of life is a life that is spent seeking and pursing the presence of the Lord.

For it is therein the Lord's presence, with this close relationship with the Lord, that a person will experience fullness of joy and pleasures forevermore.

As David concludes his Psalm in this way, it weaves all the metaphors from the previous verses together into a beautiful bow at the end.

He ties together the previous images of how God is the ultimate protector from all that threatens to harm us in life, the safest refuge. How God is the ultimate provider, the source of all goodness in life, and that apart from God there is no good. How God is the ultimate benefactor for all the riches that are bestowed upon us in life.

David weaves all these images together, and at the very end, he forms a bow as he points to how this is the path of life.

The path of life is a life spent seeking and pursuing God through a close relationship with God, and that is how we experience fullness. Or as David puts its fullness of joy with pleasures forevermore.

So, circling back to the image that I had you recall at the beginning of our sermon.

What moment in life made you feel most satisfied? At what point throughout your years have you felt the most contentment, the most satiated, the most satisfied? Was it Anything that pertained to your relationship with God? Was it an experience or some form of Goodness that God had so graciously bestowed upon you?

Our Psalm this morning from beginning to end urges us to find our satisfaction, our fullness in God.

As you know Thanksgiving is the season where we Americans gorge ourselves on all the Thanksgiving fixin's. We gorge ourselves on mashed potatoes and gravy, sweet potato casserole, stuffing, gigantic turkeys, rolls and cranberry. There is always enough to feed an army.

On thanksgiving the average American will consume close to 3,000 calories at dinner alone. That is not adding in breakfast lunch or a midnight snack. And that is also not including drinks, desserts, or appetizers with your thanksgiving meal. If you add in apps, drinks and desserts than the thanksgiving meal totals about 4,500 calories.

As westerners, our thanksgiving tradition entails inhaling as much thanksgiving fixings as possible.

Well, let's talk about the after effects. The after effects include an overdoes on tryptophan, which in turn creates a lethargy and the post dinner nap ensues.

The desserts cause the same effect as well. The deserts cause a spike in blood sugar, which in turn causes a sugar crash and a nap is needed.

Or the overall mass inhalation of 3,000-4,500 calories causes a person to have to go take a nap as the food coma sets in.

And this sort of overindulgence is not solely pursuant with the thanksgiving season. As westerners, this tends to be our mentality regarding most things in life.

As westerners, we love to have more, more, and more. We gorge ourselves on many different things.

We gorge ourselves on things like social media, video games, and shopping for material goods, or whatever else seems to satisfy or pacify our wants at the time.

But I say all this to illustrate what happens when we gorge ourselves on things like food, social media, and material items and seek our fullness outside of, or apart from our relationship with God.

When we seek fullness apart from outside of our relationship with God then we never truly get full.

That is the whole premise of our Psalm, right?

But in turn, what it does to us, the after-effects, makes us less able to serve. It prevents us from being able to freely move around and serve God.

Just to parse this out a little bit further and give you a more well-rounded image of what I mean, I will share with you what one author had to say on this topic on the topic of gorging we on things other than God and how that has a direct correlation on how we can serve God.

He said:

People sometimes fast to make room for other things. For instance, in skipping a meal we make time to pray or serve. In shutting off technology, social media, the tv, or our smart phones then we are more available to family and friends. In reducing our overindulgence in material goods and spending, then we have more to give away.

He makes the point in this book that we fast as a way of practicing self-denial. That we deny ourselves, so that our appetites don't consume us, and we are better able to serve.

Friends, considering the stewardship season we are amidst, juxtaposed with the thanksgiving season ahead this week, I encourage you to think about the ways in which you may be overindulging in life.

I encourage you to spend some time really thinking about the areas of your life where you may be seeking to find fullness, contentment, or satisfaction outside of, or apart from, your relationship with God.

I encourage you to take an investigatory look at these things. To explore how it may be hindering your ability to be a good steward. How it is holding you back from being able to serve in a better capacity.

I encourage you to ask this question and on a continual basis: What difference might it make if we began to ground our pleasure and joy not in self, nor in stuff, but rather in God and serving others.

As our Psalmist reminded us this morning, "Our fullness is found in God."

As we seek a life pursuing God, pursuing the true path of life, there is a fullness of joy, a satisfaction and contentment that cannot be found elsewhere.

But as we seek this fullness in God then it in-turn frees us up, so we are better able to serve others with what we have so generously been given from God.

In the name of the Father, the Son and the Holy Spirit. Amen.

The Jericho Road
Luke 10:25-37

The parable of the Good Samaritan is well known to us. We can quickly recall the story as soon as we hear the title.

The problem with a commonly known parable is that the minute I start reading it, your ears close and your minds shut down. Almost immediately your attention goes elsewhere. Mostly, that is because we have heard it a million times, and we know how the story ends. We think we already have that one figured out and have gleaned all the necessary wisdom from it.

And in the case of this story, we think we know the moral of the story is to help other people. To reach out to those who are hurting and marginalized this world.

We know that this is the story of the Good Samaritan who reached out and helped his neighbor in need, and it serves as an example, for all Christians, about how we are to treat our neighbors.

I wonder if that is all that Jesus was getting at with this parable, though? Was he only offering us a parable to remind us that we are to stop and help those in need?

Was Jesus just giving us a parable to make us feel guilty when we don't stop and help others, or when we ignore a homeless person on the street?

I think that Jesus was going a little bit deeper with this one. I think that this parable presents a bigger challenge to us. The bigger challenge is to understand the depth of what coming to the aid of another entails, and what it calls us to do.

In this parable the bigger picture, the bigger challenge, is in understanding what the Jericho Road is and choosing to accept the invitation to walk the Jericho Road, with love and compassion and mercy!

In ancient times the Jericho Road was a stretch of about 20 miles that connected Jerusalem to Jericho. The Jericho road drops about 3,600 feet in that stretch of 20 miles, which makes this road very difficult to walk because of its dramatic shift in elevation. The Jericho Road is a long, steep, and winding remote road.

In addition to the Jericho Road being so steep and winding and difficult to walk, for centuries robberies and assaults took place on it.

For centuries, the Jericho road was 20 miles of violence and oppression—a strip of suffering where there were always threats of bandits.

Today the Jericho Road is a symbol or a metaphor for us. People may not traverse this steep and winding road in the Middle East as often anymore, risking their lives to do so. But we have our own present-day Jericho roads that people still walk, and they are just as dangerous, and they are just as steep and winding.

Our present-day Jericho Roads any place where people are robbed. Where people are robbed of their dignity, robbed of their love, robbed of their food and clothing, or robbed of their value and self-worth as human beings. Our Jericho Road is any place where there is suffering and oppression or where there is pain and hurting people.

In this parable we find an invitation. It is an invitation to walk the Jericho Road or we have the option to choose to decline the invitation and find a different route.

However, with this invitation to walk the Jericho there comes a caveat—we must walk it with love and compassion and mercy.

In our story we encountered four men who were walking the Jericho Road. The first man was attacked by robbers, stripped of everything, brutally beaten, and then left for dead.

The second man who was walking the Jericho Road was a Priest. Who despite his vocation in life, passed the beaten man by.

The third man who was walking the Jericho Road was a Levite. Who did the same and passed by the brutally beaten man.

Both the Priest and the Levite went to great lengths to avoid this man who had been left for dead, to the point where both of them crossed over to the other side of the road to avoid him and to avoid any further trouble.

But then there was the Samaritan who was walking along the Jericho Road, who didn't pass this man by.

The Samaritan drew close to the man who had been beaten nearly to death, and he was moved by compassion. Seeing that the man was still alive, he poured oil on him to cleanse the wound and gave him wine to dull the pain. He picked the man up and carried him on his back to the Inn. There at the Inn he promised to return and pay whatever money was owed for the man's stay.

The Samaritan in this parable was truly walking the Jericho Road. He had accepted the invitation to walk this dangerous road with love and compassion and mercy.

I saw a Facebook post recently which was a picture that a colleague of mine had posted.

In the image it is divided into two parts the top half of the picture is a snap shot of Tom Hanks from the movie *Apollo 13*. Tom Hanks has all his astronaut gear on and a head set on, so he can communicate to the control center in Houston.

Tom Hanks has a very startled and alarmed look on his face because this is taken from the scene in the movie when there were several explosions on the spaceship that had led to a series of warning lights indicating a loss of energy. Below this image of Tom Hanks, you see the popular quote, *Houston we have a problem*.

Then in the second half of the picture you see Ed Harris. Ed Harris played the role of flight director and lead contact in the control center in this movie.

Ed Harris is communicating with Tom Hanks from the control center in Houston and from that control center with all the Nasa officials he responds to Tom Hanks life threatening situation by saying, "Sending thoughts and prayers!" As in, I hope that works out for Ya. There is nothing I can do.

The point of this picture that is floating around Facebook is to generate awareness about what our world has been reduced to. In a lot of ways, the world in which we live has adopted a hands-off approach.

When someone we know is going through a difficult time or is in a crisis, we often just send them a text or an email or a Facebook post that says sending thoughts and prayers, instead of calling that person directly or instead of showing up at that person's door and asking, "What can I do to help."

In the face of tragedy and natural disasters we like to write checks to organizations who are working in those areas, instead of going to those remote places ourselves and doing the necessary manual labor ourselves. We resist going there and meeting the people personally who have just had their lives devastated.

In a lot of ways our human interactions have been reduced to a text, or an email, rather than a personal phone call, or face-to-face interactions and personal contact. It has been reduced to telling someone you are thinking about them during their difficult time, rather than showing up personally and helping to take care of them.

Mother Teresa was known as an angel of mercy. She gave her entire life to the poor, the sick, and the hungry of Calcutta India. Mother Teresa was 100% hands-on.

She began with an open-air school for homeless children and as funds came in, she expanded her work to create her order known as "The Missionaries of Charity". This charity she created focused on loving and caring for those nobody wanted to care for. She said her focus was "to help the poor and to better their lot."

Through that charity she created Shisha Bhavan, a home for babies whose parents couldn't or wouldn't care for.

She started a colony for lepers called Shanti Nagar where lepers could build homes and work in the fields.

She created Nirmal Hridhay, a home for the dying and on the very first day for that home, she picked up a woman who was literally half eaten by rats and ants and carried her to this home.

Mother Teresa understood what the Jericho Road was, and what it entailed to walk it, and she most certainly accepted the invitation to walk that road with love and compassion and mercy.

To walk the Jericho Road means we put into action everything that Jesus has taught us. It means we embody the gospel. It means that God's spirit moves within our hearts, and love and grace, mercy and compassion flow out of us.

To walk the Jericho road entails hands-on, radical and inconvenient love. It entails living outside of our comfort zone. It means exerting ourselves physically, emotionally, and financially until we are utterly exhausted from the journey.

Now we know, there is a little bit of the Priest and the Levite within each of us. We know that often we feel as if it might be easier to pass someone by instead of carrying them on our back, pouring our oil on them, sharing our wine with them, and spending our money on them, so they can be nursed back to good health at an inn.

And there may be a little bit of Ed Harris in us. Where it may be easier and more convenient to address a person's needs by sending a text that says sending thoughts and prayers.

But I truly believe there is a little bit of the Samaritan in all of us too. There must be, because we all have the Holy Spirit living within us. We all have God within us—the very source of love and compassion and mercy.

The challenge then is to let the Samaritan within each of us rise above the Priest, and the Levite, and the Ed Harris within.

We may not have the answers and solutions for all the terrible things that happen in this world like the violence and pain that is suffered on the Jericho Roads throughout our nation and our world, but what we do know is that sending thoughts and prayers, is good and all, but that isn't enough.

It takes embodying the gospel on every level and truly loving your neighbor at a whole other depth. It entails traversing those steep and dangerous and remote roads that we don't want to walk along, but we do it anyway with love and compassion and mercy.

This parable is about helping your neighbor in need, but it goes far beyond that. The challenge in this parable is to re-define loving your neighbor as yourself more radically where you adopt a hands-on approach, where you don't pass anyone by because it is uncomfortable or inconvenient. Where you don't just simply send a text that says sending thoughts and prayers.

The challenge is to answer Jesus' call at the depth in which he is calling. The Challenge is to walk the steep, winding, remote and dangerous, Jericho Roads of our present day lives with God's love and compassion and mercy pouring out of us every step of the way!

In the name of the Father, the Son and the Holy Spirit. Amen!

The Lord of All
Acts 10:34-43

Easter Sunday

In the Book of Acts, we experience our Easter message through the eyes of Peter. Peter was the one speaking in the passage and he was actually delivering a sermon, to a man named Cornelius.

Peter's words are important to us on this Easter Sunday, insofar as they summarize the entire story of Jesus—his life, ministry, death and resurrection.

However, the deeper significance in this passage resides in the mere fact that these two men, Peter and Cornelius, were interacting with one another to begin with. Cornelius was Peter's greatest adversary.

Peter was a Jewish fisherman. A leader for Christ. Cornelius was a captain in the Roman army, the entity that fought tirelessly to destroy Christ, and furthermore Cornelius was a Gentile.

One of the greatest conflicts of the 1st century was the Jewish-Gentile conflict. Most of the early believers were Jewish-Christians, and it was the Gentiles who served as the greatest barrier to spreading the Good News of Christ.

They fought against anyone who followed Christ and persecuted them. So, most Jews avoided Gentiles. It was scandalous to associate with them.

But here Peter is, as one of the front runners for Christ, a devote Jew standing in the living room of a Gentile's home. Better yet standing in a Roman army official's living room teaching him about Christ.

While this may have initially been an uncomfortable and awkward situation for the two men, something that neither one of them ever foresaw happening, it ended up having a life-changing effect on the both of them.

What ended up happening in Cornelius's home that day was a new chapter was written in Christian history. A new chapter was written where a Jewish Christian leader and a Gentile-Roman army captain became friends, as Cornelius converted to Christianity. What happened that day was two men entered a home as adversaries and left as brothers in Christ.

What ended up unfolding in that living room was perhaps one of the greatest revelations of the 1st century. It was the revelation that in Christ there is no separation. It was the realization that there is no longer Jew or Gentile. For all are one, in Christ.

The apostle Paul wrote about this very thing in his letter to the Galatians when he said, "In Christ, there is no longer Jew or Gentile, slave or free, male or female, for all are one."

That is the crux of this passage. God shows no partiality, He is the Lord of all people!

And for Peter, he got to experience the power of that impartiality first hand as it united him with someone, he had thought was his greatest enemy and adversary.

In this unique rendering of our Easter story, God is making it clear for us that the Good News of Christ is for everyone. That the Lord is the Lord of all people.

It's a reminder that for Christ there exists no barriers due to race, ethnicity, culture, language, geography, or economic level. There are no barriers due to political affiliations or biases, or denominational preferences.

There is a universal love that unites all of us together!

There is an agency I used to volunteer with up in Buffalo, NY called PATH. It's a non-profit agency that works to eliminate the human trafficking issue in the world. The agency is a safe place where victims of human trafficking, or any sort of exploitation, can go and find help. They can get connected with community resources and receive counseling and care.

There are all sorts of women that are involved with this agency. Some are from the Buffalo area who became involved with prostitution and needed help, so they sought out this agency for help and protection.

Some are from other countries and are seeking asylum. Each woman has a unique story. And most of the stories are just plain horrific; they're mind-blowing and bring you to tears.

A couple weeks ago when I was there, I had the opportunity to lead a Bible study with the ladies. Within the group of ladies participating in this bible study, there were two women who were Muslim, one of them was from Pakistan, and the other one was from Syria.

There was a woman from the Congo, and two other women originally from the Congo who had been living in D.C. but had been relocated to Buffalo. And one woman was from Florida.

They were from all walks of life. There were various ethnicities, some significant cultural differences, religious affiliations and denominational preferences, as well as a couple of language barriers to overcome.

In order to overcome the language barriers, we had to get a translator for the three women from Congo, who translated everything I was saying into French. We had another translator for the women who were from Pakistan and Syria, who translated everything I was saying into Arabic for them.

At that point I began the Bible study, and I began by reading a passage from Luke. I read the passage aloud in English and listened as it was immediately translated into French and Arabic. As I heard it translated in two languages, I just sat there amazed. I sat there in amazement as I listened to the word of God, being spoken in several different languages at once.

I continued with the Bible study and spoke about how God is our protector and provider—our refuge, and as it was translated, I watched these women from all over the world, with various backgrounds, and cultures, and various life experiences, nod their heads with conviction and in agreement.

During this time of Bible study, we all shared stories of how God had personally touched our lives, brought us through tough times of tremendous heartache and had cared for each of us.

And at the end of the Bible study, I asked for prayer requests. If they had anything they needed or wanted me to pray about, for them.

I listened to the requests of the women, and their heartbreaking prayers, and their deepest woes. Things that you and I will never have to experience in our lives. Then we all joined hands and prayed together.

I prayed in English while it was translated into French and Arabic, and I ended our prayer by saying and all God's children said, "Amen," and all are various accents joined together to say, "Amen".

The Lord is the Lord of all People. God breaks down any and all barriers due to race, ethnicity, culture, language, geography, and even religious affiliation. For in God, there is no partiality we are all one.

This is exactly what Peter was preaching about in our passage from Acts. That is exactly what Peter encountered in his own personal life with Cornelius, as he became brothers in Christ with his greatest adversary. Someone of a different religious belief.

This is the message for each of us on Easter. A message about God's impartial and universal love for all of humanity.

Included with our Easter message about God's deep love for all His people, comes an admonishment from Peter to carry forth Christ's message of peace, unity, and impartiality out into the world.

At the end of our reading in Acts, Peter reminds us that we are commanded to preach and to testify to people. To witness to others about Christ. It is an admonishment to continue doing the work of Christ in this world.

Essentially it is an admonishment to desire a relationship with all kinds of people just as Christ did. To love all people just as Christ did, and to make peace with all people *because Christ did.*

I attended a lecture by the Dalai Lama one time. During this lecture the Dalai Lama spoke about human compassion and he started out by saying:

> Humans lack a sense of compassion and overall lack a general concern for one another. Humans divide themselves based on eye color, wealth, religion, education, and many more things.

He said, "We could change the whole world, if we just realized our oneness. If we just focused on the fact that we are all born into this world breathing air, we all need food to survive, we all have hair on our heads." He pointed to his bald head and said, "some of us have more hair than others though."

And then he said, "We are all human and to look at our commonalities instead of our differences would increase our human compassion for one another. It would change the world by uniting us."

When Christ was arrested, He was sentenced to death for sharing this same type of message about a universal love, and an expansive peace that has the power to unite the entire human race.

Christ was trying to reconcile the world, create peace, and harmony for all people, but the world wasn't ready to hear that. They couldn't receive that message. Powerful entities felt threatened by it, and they fought against it and Him.

The beauty of Easter is that the message of love and peace that Jesus was spreading didn't die. It was resurrected as Jesus was resurrected.

And because it was resurrected God has entrusted each of us, as Christ's disciples, with the mission of carrying that message out into our world.

We live in a day and age when this message is needed most. This world is in serious need of some peace and harmony.

I am sure you all have heard the recent news regarding the latest terrorist attack in Brussels. In President Obama's response to that devastating attack he stated, "This is just one more reason why the world needs to unite".

Let us remember that God breaks down all barriers, even political barriers. We live in a day and age where Christ's message of peace and unity needs to be shared by all and reconciliation truly sought after.

And when Christ died, it became our duty and mission to carry forth His message of peace and to love all people, to break down any barriers that threaten to separate us and to unite this world.

We are reminded that God is the Lord of all people. We are reminded that God shows no partiality, and He breaks down barriers of all kinds.

We are reminded that through the power of this impartiality, we can all be united.

This is the message we have been entrusted with. It is now up to us to carry it out into our world.

In the name of the Father, the Son, and the Holy Spirit. Amen.

The Power of Forgiveness
Genesis 45:1-15; Matthew 15:10-20

Last Sunday we heard the beginning of Joseph's story. We heard about how Joseph's brothers hated him. How they hated him so much that they plotted against him and eventually sold Joseph into slavery.

This week we heard the end of Joseph's story where he came face-to-face with his brothers after many years of being apart.

In between these two bookends a lot transpired.

Joseph spent twenty-two years separated from his family. He spent several years in prison, and he spent many years working as a slave as Potiphar's servant, which eventually led to Joseph rising to the top and becoming the second most powerful man in Egypt. Even though Joseph's story turned out well, as he rose to power, it is still a tragic tale in many ways.

It's tragic tale in the sense that Joseph spent so many years separated from his father, whom he loved and adored. It's tragic in the sense that he had such a tarnished relationship with his brothers. It's tragic in the sense that he had to spend time in prison, and then working as a slave.

During those many years that Joseph spent working as a slave and was confined in prison, he could have kept a fire of fury burning within him over his circumstances. It could have erupted into an explosion of anger at the first sight of his brothers.

However, at the initial sighting of his siblings, he did the opposite of what we would have expected him to do. Instead of acting out of rage, hostility, bitterness, or resentment, Joseph demonstrated grace and mercy, love and forgiveness.

At the initial sight of his brothers, Joseph broke down in tears to the point that his weeping became so loud that it echoed all throughout the house. Then he approached his brothers

He approached his brothers and told them to not be scared or distressed. To not be angry with themselves for what they had done to him. Joseph chose to forgive them. What he did next was even more surprising. He not only forgave them for what they did to him, but he told them he would take care of them.

They had already spent two years going through the famine, and he knew they didn't have what they needed to survive the remaining years of famine. So, he told them to return to their farms, gather their wives and children, even their flocks and herds, and to return to Egypt.

He promised to take them in, and he would make sure they had everything they needed, in order to survive the rest of the famine, so they would never face poverty or destitution.

Joseph could have crushed his brothers. He could have tortured them. He could have really taught them a lesson and repaid them for what they had done to him. He was powerful enough to do so, but instead, Joseph chose forgiveness.

He chose to extend kindness and mercy, and he chose to extend love and grace to them.

For most of us, we would not have responded the same way Joseph did. We would have struggled with forgiving them. I am not so sure I would take someone in who had sold me into slavery, which leaves me wondering (and I think it leaves most people wondering): "How did he do that?"

How did Joseph look his brothers in the eyes, after such an atrocity and choose to extend grace and forgiveness to them? I think the answer to how Joseph was able to do this lies somewhere in between our bookends.

It lies somewhere in between those chapters from last week, to this week. In between those years that Joseph spent separated from his brothers and family.

The answer lies in the fact that Joseph had spent twenty-two years grieving, and mourning, and really wrestling with what happened, which gradually over time gave way for forgiveness to slowly take root in his heart.

The Joseph story spans 14 chapters. Throughout those 14 chapters there are several instances that detail Joseph's grieving process. In Genesis 42 we are told of a time when Joseph hurried away from the crowds and went into this room privately, to weep.

Again, in Genesis 43 Joseph is performing his routine servant duties by serving a meal and he breaks down to the point of tears during the middle of it all. After quite some time, he is eventually able to compose himself.

I am sure that throughout those twenty-two years between the time he was sold into slavery by his brothers, to the time that he came face-to-face again with his brothers, he was able to grieve and mourn and to process what had happened.

Little by little, forgiveness was able to slowly creep in and take root in his heart.

Forgiveness is a hard thing to accomplish sometimes. It is hard to truly forgive someone whom we feel has wronged us. To forgive someone when they have caused us so much pain and heartbreak, or when our family members or loved ones have caused so much pain and agony. Often times forgiveness doesn't seem practical or even rational. There are times when forgiveness seems like a distant reality and just a nice idea on Sunday morning.

When we choose to not forgive is when the resentment, the bitterness, and the fury starts to take root in our hearts.

That is when we let the pain and the anger have all the power, to the point that it burrows into our bones until it eventually furrows in our souls, and we start acting and responding out of those deep wounds.

When we allow that to happen, we are only hurting ourselves.

The Tower of London is a royal palace and a historical castle located in central London. In the oldest part of the Tower of London, there is something referred to as, The Little Ease. The Little Ease is an old dungeon, and ironically enough, it is situated in the Tower of London directly below the Chapel of St. John.

This infamous dungeon was a torture cell in the early 13th century and remained an active torture cell well into the 16th century. In fact, during the reign of Henry the 8th, it was utilized the most.

The reason it was called the Little Ease was due to its tiny size. It measures a mere 4 feet by feet. Its cramped size prevented prisoners from settling into any sort of bearable position. It prevented them from being able to stand, sit or lie down.

Furthermore, this windowless cell was in constant blackness. So, the inhabitants of it who were being tortured were forced to crouch in solitary confinement for days or even a week before they were eventually released for interrogation.

Frederick Buechner, famous theologian and Presbyterian minister draws parallels between the dungeon known as the Little Ease and forgiveness, in this way.

He says, "It's oak door blocks out all light and all ventilation. It measures only 4 feet square and 4 feet high. There is no way either to stand upright in it, or to lie down at full length. We know it as The Little Ease, but to live an unforgiving life of restricted mercy is to live in that dark, airless, crippling place where there is no ease at all.

In that place where we feel only our wounds. Where we hear only our heart's beat with rage." He says, "it is in that place where we will be damned, before we forgive and forget. And that is exactly what we are."

There is no escape from bitterness, hatred, and violence. There is no chance for healing and peace without forgiveness. Unresolved anger leads to bitterness, hostility, and revenge.

Forgiveness, on the other hand, leads to freedom and reconciliation.

There is no character in Genesis that better illustrates the fundamentals of forgiveness, then Joseph. There is no chapter which more clearly defines and describes the essentials of forgiveness, than our passage this morning.

In this passage, Joseph falls on his brother's neck, he weeps tears that billow throughout his household. They are tears of love and grace, tears of mercy and acceptance; they are tears of forgiveness.

Joseph's story is the pinnacle of what it looks like to forgive and to free yourself from anger, bitterness and resentment.

There are some abominable events that have made headline news recently. There are just down right terrible atrocities that have occurred as of late.

The incident in Charlottesville. The terrorist attack in Barcelona. Then the terrorist attack in Carbis just to rattle off a few.

There are acts of violence, bigotry, racism, national threats, and homicides happening every day, all throughout this country and numerous other.

In the face of all this, I go back to my initial question regarding Joseph's story: How did he do that? How did Joseph choose forgiveness?

Furthermore, how do we do that? How do we choose grace and forgiveness in the face of such atrocities?

We have already identified from Joseph's story that it takes time. It takes time to heal, it takes time to process, and it takes time to forgive.

It perhaps took Joseph every minute of those twenty-two years for forgiveness to truly penetrate his heart and take root.

So, what does a person do in the mean time? What do we do when we haven't been moved yet to that place where we can extend forgiveness?

And that is when we turn to Jesus' example. We turn to Jesus' example when he hung dying on the cross, for both my sins and your sins, and still cried out for God to forgive them. "Forgive them Father, for they know not what they do."

Jesus knew that forgiveness was the only way to emotional and spiritual freedom. Jesus knew there was power in forgiveness

He also knew it was not a natural human impulse, which is why he left us with his example, and with his own words for us to fall back on, and to rely on when we falter.

We know that forgiveness is not an easy task, but if we say some acts are just too much to forgive, then we renounce God's infinite capacity *to forgive us.*

If we refuse to forgive because the cost to our pride and wellbeing is too great, then we reject the ultimate cost Christ paid for us on the cross.

And it is at that point that we place ourselves in a dark, airless, crippling prison cell where we are doing nothing more than torturing ourselves.

Archbishop Desmond Tutu once preached: "Forgiving means abandoning your right to pay back the perpetrator in his own coin; but it is a loss that liberates the victim."

Hearing this when Nelson Mandela became the first Black president of South Africa, he chose reconciliation instead of revenge to end years of Apartheid.

The late Pope John Paul II was nearly killed in 1981 by a Turkish gunman. Two years later he sat in a prison cell outside Rome with his would-be assassin.

He reached out, took the hand that had held the gun meant to take his life, then he spoke to this man a word of forgiveness.

Forgiveness is difficult. It is complicated, and it is gritty, but there is power in it.

Forgiveness does not necessarily mean that we forgive our perpetrator and then go back to living in a loving relationship with them. In many instances it may entail walking away from that person forever.

Forgiveness does not mean that we tolerate cruel or life-threatening behavior or forget brutalities that should be remembered so we learn from them.

Forgiveness in its simplest form means that we simply don't let the anger, the hurt, the pain, the bitterness and resentment have all the power and take root in our hearts.

So, friends, in those moments when forgiveness is the furthest thing from your heart or mind, when it is a far distant reality and just seems like a nice idea on a Sunday morning, choose it anyway.

Choose to free yourself from the dark, airless, crippling prison cell.

And in that moment of forgiveness, if you simply cannot find your own words of forgiveness to speak, rely on the words that Jesus left us with when he said:

Forgive them Father.

Forgive them Father for they know not what they do.

In the name of the Father, the Son, and the Holy Spirit. Amen.

www.ingramcontent.com/pod-product-compliance
Lightning Source LLC
Chambersburg PA
CBHW052200110526
44591CB00012B/2019